POETRY FOR THE PRESIDENT— IN GOD WE TRUST

POETRY FOR THE PRESIDENT— IN GOD WE TRUST

BILLIE JO BALDWIN

To order additional copies of this book, contact:
Xlibris Corporation
1-888-795-4274
www.Xlibris.com
Orders@Xlibris.com
34216

INTRODUCTION

When Solomon died in 931 B.C., the eighty year monarchy of he and his father David ended, and the two primary contributors to the poetry and wisdom literature of Israel passed from the scene. Therefore, before beginning, the reign of Rehoboam at the division of the kingdom, we will consider this body of literature. The poetic books include Job, Psalms, Proverbs, Ecclesiastes and Song of Solomon. David was the primary contributor to the Psalms and Solomon wrote many proverbs, as well as being the author of Ecclesiastes and Song of Solomon.

In ancient times, the wise men wrestled with two basic questions: 1. The basic problems of life; namely pain, suffering and why evil seems to prosper, (or why individuals involved in evil-doing seem to prosper). 2. The concept of how to live out life with skill. It may be said that the problems people face today have not changed since 1000 B.C. If you ask individuals on the street today what they are concerned with, they say: "What is the purpose of life? Why is there pain and suffering? Why is it that I see evil people prospering while I live right and never seem to succeed?" In this regard, nothing has changed for three thousand years.

In the book of Proverbs, Ecclesiastes and Job, these questions can be satisfied. In the book of Psalms and in the Song of Solomon, we find expressions of poetry in its highest form following the ancient Hebrew motif.

Messianic Psalms

Our study of Psalms would not be complete without consideration of the Messianic Psalms. These are Psalms concerned with the Messiah. They were Given to the Psalmist by the Lord Jesus Christ in his pre-incarnate eternal state. As the Lord Jesus looked down throughout the corridors of time from eternity past, He poured out his heart in anticipation of the sufferings and sorrows that he knowingly faced for us. Many Messianic Psalms were written by David Between 1010 and 970 B.C., one thousand years before the crucifixion and resurrection of the Lord Jesus Christ.

―――――――――――

Typical

There are three types of Messianic Psalms. The first can be identified as typical. In a typical Messianic Psalm there is some feature in the life of the Psalmist that is intended by the holy spirit to be a picture or type of the Coming Messiah. Some particular feature or aspect of his life, or some characteristic of the individual, or something he does or experience, is a type of Messiah. In the typical Messianic Psalm, we do not say that all the Psalmist's life, activities, or circumstances mentioned, are messianic. Otherwise, in many instances we would end up with heresy. Only some particular feature of the Psalm is the Type. Psalm 69 is an ideal example. Psalm 69 is a lament, or reminder, Psalm. Verse 5 demonstrates that the entire Psalm is not Messianic. It reads, "O God, thou knowest my foolishness; and my sins are not hid from thee." We know this cannot refer to the Messiah because He was sinless. But then in verse 7 we read, "because for thy sake I have borne reproach; shame hath covered my face." With that, David's experience becomes a type of the Messiah. He continues in verse 8, "I am become a stranger unto my brethren, and an alien unto my mother's children." Notice the synonymous parallelism in these two verses. Again, David's experience made him a type of Christ, who in his lifetime became a stranger and an alien because his relatives believed he was "beside himself."

Continuing in Psalm 69, verse 9 says, "For the zeal of thine house hath eaten me up." As a theocentric individual, David was so consumed with the worship of Jehovah, that he spent hours and days in worship at the ark in Jerusalem and at the tabernacle and brazen in Gibeon. In this Psalm he said, "I am just consumed with God; I am consumed with worshiping God." A thousand years later, when the Apostle John saw the Lord Jesus in his zeal for the temple, he recorded in John 2:17, "and his disciples remembered that it was written, the zeal of thine house hath eaten me up." In that respect, they immediately likened the Lord Jesus to his ancestor David and linked him with this Psalm. Again, in verse 12, David's experience is a type of Christ: "they that sit in the gate speak against me; and I was the song of the drunkards." Look at verse 19 and 20:

> Thou has know my reproach, and my shame, and my dishonour: . . . .
> Reproach hath broken my heart; and I am full of heaviness; and I looked for some to take pity, but there was none; and for comforters, but I found none.

As the Lord Jesus Christ was on the cross one thousand years later, looking at the faces staring up at him, he saw them shooting out the lip, wagging their heads, mocking him and saying, "THOU SON OF GOD come down from the cross and save thyself," as the Psalmist said, he found no pity in any of the eyes or faces looking up at him in sullen pride and arrogance.

Typical Prophetic

Finally, in verse 21, the Psalmist says, "They gave me also gall for my meat; and in my thirst they gave me vinegar to drink." We have no evidence that this ever happened to David. Therefore, when he uses this kind of vocabulary, he steps beyond the category of a Typical Messianic Psalm, and moves into the category of a Typical-Prophetic Messianic Psalm. Up to this point, history has been in play in David's life. He experienced the rebuke of his friends when he fled from Saul, and was abused by Shimei when he fled from Absalom. When he was across the Jordan after Absalom had invaded Jerusalem, I am certain he was the song of the drunkards, and even later on during the rebellion of Sheba. So, in those portions of the Psalm, David was experiencing in his own life those things that the Lord Jesus would later experience. I do not believe that David ever experienced the gall and the vinegar. So, we Find that in a Typical-Prophetic Messianic Psalm, that history is not the only force in play. In the Typical-Prophetic Messianic Psalm, the Psalmist's vocabulary goes beyond his personal experiences and he begins to express ideas and occurrences which he never encountered or experiences himself.

I do not know what the Psalmist thought as he wrote such words under the inspiration of the Holy Spirit. He may have believed it was figurative language. But the figurative language, and what may sometimes have even appeared to be hyperbole was literally fulfilled in the Lord Jesus Christ. So the definition for a Typical-Prophetic Messianic Psalm is history plus inspired foresight, with the Psalmist going beyond himself and his own experience.

Example of Psalm 22

Much of the center of thought in the Messianic Psalms has to do with the sufferings of the Lord Jesus. Which of us can really know the sufferings of crucifixion? Certainly I do not. But we do know it was agony beyond compare. We do have a Hollywood stereotype of crucifixion. We have seen a tall cross standing high above the horizon in many of the films. In reality, this was not the case. The roman cross was short. In fact, the victim of crucifixion was rarely more than two feet above the ground. While the victim remained alive, the wild dogs would come in from the desert and chew on his legs. Very often, a victim of crucifixion would live for two or three days in agony. During crucifixion, the victim was first placed on the cross which was lying on the ground. Nails were driven through the hands at the juncture of the wrist, and then through the feet to secure him in that position. The cross was then raised and dropped into a previously dug hole. When it struck the bottom of the hole, the impact would usually pull loose the shoulder joints and ligaments, as the entire body weight pulled against the wrist with the force of the cross being dropped. In this distended position, diaphragmic action was immediately reduced. Breathing became shallow and as the victim sank lower, he began to suffocate. In order to breathe, and to relieve the pain in his hands, he would push himself back up with his feet. But, this action caused the pain in his feet to be so excruciating, that he would again sag to relieve it. As this agonizing cycle continued, the victim began to take on a grotesque zigzag, letter z position, with the body skewed to one side and the knees pointed out in the opposite direction. As death began to creep slowly on him, a semi rigor mortis set in. Because of the loss of diaphragmatic action, and the fact that the bones were pulled out of joint, the victim began to not only suffocate, but also to become extremely thirsty. Add to that the fact that he was impaled naked and helpless for all to see. It was a pain, agony, and humiliation beyond compare. And, if that were not sufficient, the Lord Jesus suffered with a crown of thorns and a mutilated back as he bore our sins there on Calvary's tree. Yet, we could wish him no greater diadem, than that crown of thorns because our minds go back to the curse in the Garden of Eden, when God said that nature would bring forth thorns as a result of Adam's fall. Then they made the crown of thorns and pressed it on the head of the Saviour, he hung there suspended between heaven and earth. And, with the blood streaming down his forehead, the thorny diadem had great significance. He was bearing the curse for all mankind and all of creation, as he performed the act of redemption. The scripture is very plain when it says, "It pleased the Lord to bruise him"(Isa. 53:10). Because he was a lamb slain from before the foundation of the world, in anticipation of his agony to be endured for our sakes, Christ opened his heart to the Psalmist as he penned in Psalm 22:1, "My God, my God, why hast thou forsaken me? Why art thou so far from helping me?" David was in desperate trouble when he penned this, and the Messiah would be in more desperate trouble when he used those words as he was on the cross.

> Verse 7: all they that see me laugh me to scorn: they shoot
> Out the lip, they shake the head.
> 14: I am poured out like water, and all my bones are
> out of joint: and my heart is like wax.

As the Lord Jesus looked down at himself, hanging suspended on the cross with all of his ribs visible, his breathing becoming shallow, he said, "My bones are out of joint." Look at verse 16: "they pierced my hands and my feet." There is no historical record that David ever had his hands and feet pierced. As he penned this, he must have wondered what he was saying; but a thousand years later the Lord Jesus literally experienced this. The prophecy continues in verse 18: "They part my, garments among them, and cast lots for my vesture." In no way can this be historical. It is prophecy as Christ himself inspired David to write what he would experience when he paid the ultimate penalty for sin on Calvary's cross.

Prophetic Psalm

The third type of Messianic Psalm is one which is completely prophetic. Psalm. 110 is an example of this type. The Lord Jesus quoted from it to prove that he was the Messiah. In Matthew 22:41ff, we read, while the Pharisees were gathered together, Jesus asked them, saying, what think ye of Christ? Whose son is he? They say unto him, the son of David. He saith unto them, how then doth David in the spirit call him Lord, saying, the Lord said unto my Lord, sit thou on my right hand, till I make thine enemies thy footstool? If David then call him Lord, how is he his son?

His enemies were so confounded they did not say a word to challenge him from that time forward. Read Psalm 110:1: "The Lord said unto my Lord, Sit thou at my right hand, until I make thine enemies thy footstool." As king over Israel, David was the world's number one man, answerable only to God. This is the crux of the question. How could David have a Lord between himself and God? Literally what David was saying in Psalm 110:1 was, "The Lord said unto my liege." So David had a greater Lord, the Messiah, yet he is his son. As we look back with the benefit of the new testament, we know exactly how this could happen. But the Lord Jesus used it to confound the Pharisees because he was the greater son. Psalm 110 is a completely Prophetic Messianic Psalm. It contains no history, no historical counterpart, no typology or picture. In Psalm 110, only David's greater counterpart, Messiah, risen and ruling, is in view.

Imprecatory Psalms

One major type of Psalm remains to be considered-the imprecatory Psalm. This type demonstrates righteous indignation. In these; the Psalmist says such things as "Break out their teeth. Destroy them. Defeat them. Wreak vengeance on them." There are at least eighteen of these Psalms, containing 368 verses, of which only about seventy-five include anything that can be called in imprecation. They have long been a subject of discussion, because in them the Psalmist, under the inspiration of the holy spirit, calls down violence, vengeance, wrath, and revenge on the recipient of the imprecation. How does this equate with the love of God in the new testament? There are two unacceptable answers to this question.

First, they are just what they seem, the language of a heart that cries out for vengeance. In other words, they are the same kind of spirit that Moses displayed when he struck the rock twice.

Let me give three answers to the hypothesis.

1) they were composed in leisure. They were not composed in the heat of extreme provocation or anger.
2) imprecations on one's enemies should be repented of, not written down for others to read.
3) these Psalms contain in them an implicit claim that the feeling is in some sense true and right, and is one the reader can sympathize and agree with. So, for these three reasons, I believe the imprecatory Psalms are not just the language of an angry heart.

The second unacceptable answer says: the morality of the old testament is on a lower standard than that of the new testament. In the first place,

Moses forbids private vengeance and Leviticus 19:18, is an excellent example. Exodus 23:4-5, states that we are to help our enemies. Second, Paul builds his doctrine of the sin of a vengeful spirit on the old testament scriptures. You can check on this in Romans 12:19-21. Third, David was a rare man of unusual strength and character. Twice he spared the life of his mortal enemy, and finally uttered the Song of the Bow, as it is called, to commemorate him (II Sam. 1:17-27). This hardly exemplifies a low standard of morality. (As far as I am concerned, this gives the coup de grace to both views.) Fourth, notice that our Lord and his apostles quoted from these Imprecatory Psalms.

I believe the proper view of the Imprecatory Psalms rests on a variety of elements that we must take into consideration. First, these expressions contain the longing of an old testament saint for the vindication of God's righteousness. For example, David was a man of piety. He was God's anointed. Yet his enemies lived in ease, honor, and luxury, in Saul's court. Is it any wonder that David longed for a reversal of conditions that would answer all doubt concerning God's righteousness, and assure him of the reality of his anointing and future position as king?

Second, they were utterances of zeal for the kingdom of God; David was acutely conscious of the sanctity of his own anointed office. His whole life centered on serving God as king over his people. Yet at the time Saul was also anointed. David's greatest respect for this holy office prevented him from ever touching Saul. Yet because David was God's representative, his enemies were no longer his but God's. So David might ask for these people a fate in keeping with their Current state. Paul makes a similar statement in I Corinthians 16:22.

Third, the utterance in the imprecatory Psalms are the old testament expression of God's hatred of sin. David's thoughts were not chiefly against Saul or Absalom, but rather against the sycophants and political intriguers who urged them on: doeg, crush, Ahithophel, and others. It was impossible for David to differentiate between Satan and the sinner. Doctrines such as soteriology, Demonology, angelology, were not developed in his time. I believe these Psalms represent prophetic teachings concerning God's attitude toward sin and the impenitent and persistent sinner.

Fourth, I think that as a preface to our later consideration of the book of Job, we must remember that these were more simplistic times and the eastern mind looked at a person as being either under God's curse or God's blessing. From this viewpoint, one who prospered was evidently a recipient of God's blessing, while one who was suffering, was evidently under God's curse because of some sin in his life. When David, or anyone else, observed evil men prospering, they would call for God's judgment to fall on them as a vindication of God's righteousness. It was part of David's concept of, Lord, let thy name be hallowed in the earth. It is the concept of the prayer which the Lord gave to his disciples, "thy kingdom come; thy will be done." As David looked around and saw mankind in a rebellious state against God, and saw evil in the world, he knew it slandered the name of God. Even though such men were wicked, they were part of God's creation. David saw God's name being maligned, and God's character maligned, because his creation was in a state of disobedience. So he prayed: "call down judgment on them! Vindicate Your position! Destroy the evil doers so that others will see it and know that God is in heaven and he punishes evil."

THE PANORAMA OF THE OLD TESTAMENT By: Thomas R. Rogers, D. Min. TRINITY COLLEGE OF THE BIBLE THEOLOGICAL SEMINARY

Thank-You kindly to Dr. Thomas Rogers and all the staff at TRINITY COLLEGE OF THE BIBLE THEOLOGICAL SEMINARY for online course study visit *www.trinitysem.edu.Newburg.In.*

Psalm 1

1 Blessed is the man that walketh not in the counsel of the wicked, Nor standeth in the way of sinners, Nor sitteth in the seat of scoffers:

2 But his delight is in the law of Jehovah; And on his law doth he meditate day and night.

3 And he shall be like a tree planted by the streams of water, That bringeth forth its fruit in its season, Whose leaf also doth not wither; And whatsoever he doeth shall prosper.

4 The wicked are not so, But are like the chaff which the wind driveth away.

5 Therefore the wicked shall not stand in the judgment, Nor sinners in the congregation of the righteous.

6 For Jehovah knoweth the way of the righteous; But the way of the wicked shall perish.

Psalm 2

1   Why do the nations rage, And the peoples meditate a vain thing?

2   The kings of the earth set themselves, And the rulers take counsel together, Against Jehovah, and against his anointed, saying,

3   Let us break their bonds asunder, And cast away their cords from us.

4   He that sitteth in the heavens will laugh: The Lord will have them in derision.

5   Then will he speak unto them in his wrath, And vex them in his sore displeasure:

6   Yet I have set my king Upon my holy hill of Zion.

7   I will tell of the decree: Jehovah said unto me, Thou art my son; This day have I begotten thee.

8   Ask of me, and I will give thee the nations for thine inheritance, And the uttermost parts of the earth for thy possession.

9   Thou shalt break them with a rod of iron; Thou shalt dash them in pieces like a potter's vessel.

10   Now therefore be wise, O ye kings: Be instructed, ye judges of the earth.

11   Serve Jehovah with fear, And rejoice with trembling.

12   Kiss the son, lest he be angry, and ye perish in the way, For his wrath will soon be kindled. Blessed are all they that take refuge in him.

Psalm 3

A Psalm of David, when he fled from Absalom his son.

1 Jehovah, how are mine adversaries increased! Many are they that rise up against me.

2 Many there are that say of my soul, There is no help for him in God. Selah

3 But thou, O Jehovah, art a shield about me; My glory and the lifter up of my head.

4 I cry unto Jehovah with my voice, And he answereth me out of his holy hill. Selah

5 I laid me down and slept; I awaked; for Jehovah sustaineth me.

6 I will not be afraid of ten thousands of the people That have set themselves against me round about.

7 Arise, O Jehovah; save me, O my God: For thou hast smitten all mine enemies upon the cheek bone; Thou hast broken the teeth of the wicked.

8 Salvation belongeth unto Jehovah: Thy blessing be upon thy people. Selah

Psalm 4

For the Chief Musician; on stringed instruments. A Psalm of David.

1   Answer me when I call, O God of my righteousness; Thou hast set me at large when I was in distress: Have mercy upon me, and hear my prayer.

2   O ye sons of men, how long shall my glory be turned into dishonor? How long will ye love vanity, and seek after falsehood? Selah

3   But know that Jehovah hath set apart for himself him that is godly: Jehovah will hear when I call unto him.

4   Stand in awe, and sin not: Commune with your own heart upon your bed, and be still. Selah

5   Offer the sacrifices of righteousness, And put your trust in Jehovah.

6   Many there are that say, Who will show us any good? Jehovah, lift thou up the light of thy countenance upon us.

7   Thou hast put gladness in my heart, More than they have when their grain and their new wine are increased.

8   In peace will I both lay me down and sleep; For thou, Jehovah, alone makest me dwell in safety.

Psalm 5

For the Chief Musician; with the Nehiloth. A Psalm of David.

1 Give ear to my words, O Jehovah, Consider my meditation.

2 Hearken unto the voice of my cry, my King, and my God; For unto thee do I pray.

3 O Jehovah, in the morning shalt thou hear my voice; In the morning will I order my prayer unto thee, and will keep watch.

4 For thou art not a God that hath pleasure in wickedness: Evil shall not sojourn with thee.

5 The arrogant shall not stand in thy sight: Thou hatest all workers of iniquity.

6 Thou wilt destroy them that speak lies: Jehovah abhorreth the blood-thirsty and deceitful man.

7 But as for me, in the abundance of thy loving kindness will I come into thy house: In thy fear will I worship toward thy holy temple.

8 Lead me, O Jehovah, in thy righteousness because of mine enemies; Make thy way straight before my face.

9 For there is no faithfulness in their mouth; Their inward part is very wickedness; Their throat is an open sepulchre; They flatter with their tongue.

10 Hold them guilty, O God; Let them fall by their own counsels; Thrust them out in the multitude of their transgressions; For they have rebelled against thee.

[11] But let all those that take refuge in thee rejoice, Let them ever shout for joy, because thou defendest them: Let them also that love thy name be joyful in thee.

[12] For thou wilt bless the righteous; O Jehovah, thou wilt compass him with favor as with a shield.

Psalm 6

For the Chief Musician; on stringed instruments, set to the Sheminith. A Psalm of David.

1 O Jehovah, rebuke me not in thine anger, Neither chasten me in thy hot displeasure.

2 Have mercy upon me, O Jehovah; for I am withered away: O Jehovah, heal me; for my bones are troubled.

3 My soul also is sore troubled: And thou, O Jehovah, how long?

4 Return, O Jehovah, deliver my soul: Save me for thy lovingkindness' sake.

5 For in death there is no remembrance of thee: In Sheol who shall give thee thanks?

6 I am weary with my groaning; Every night make I my bed to swim; I water my couch with my tears.

7 Mine eye wasteth away because of grief; It waxeth old because of all mine adversaries.

8 Depart from me, all ye workers of iniquity; For Jehovah hath heard the voice of my weeping.

9 Jehovah hath heard my supplication; Jehovah will receive my prayer.

10 All mine enemies shall be put to shame and sore troubled: They shall turn back, they shall be put to shame suddenly.

Psalm 7

Shiggaion of David, which he sang unto Jehova, concerning the words of Cush a Benjamite.

1   O Jehovah my God, in thee do I take refuge: Save me from all them that pursue me, and deliver me,

2   Lest they tear my soul like a lion, Rending it in pieces, while there is none to deliver.

3   O Jehovah my God, if I have done this; If there be iniquity in my hands;

4   If I have rewarded evil unto him that was at peace with me; (Yea, I have delivered him that without cause was mine adversary;)

5   Let the enemy pursue my soul, and overtake it; Yea, let him tread my life down to the earth, And lay my glory in the dust. Selah

6   Arise, O Jehovah, in thine anger; Lift up thyself against the rage of mine adversaries, And awake for me; thou hast commanded judgment.

7   And let the congregation of the peoples compass thee about; And over them return thou on high.

8   Jehovah ministereth judgment to the peoples: Judge me, O Jehovah, according to my righteousness, and to mine integrity that is in me.

9   O let the wickedness of the wicked come to an end, but establish thou the righteous: For the righteous God trieth the minds and hearts.

10   My shield is with God, Who saveth the upright in heart.

11   God is a righteous judge, Yea, a God that hath indignation every day.

12   If a man turn not, he will whet his sword; He hath bent his bow, and made it ready.

13   He hath also prepared for him the instruments of death; He maketh his arrows fiery shafts.

14   Behold, he travaileth with iniquity; Yea, he hath conceived mischief, and brought forth falsehood.

15   He hath made a pit, and digged it, And is fallen into the ditch which he made.

16   His mischief shall return upon his own head, And his violence shall come down upon his own pate.

17   I will give thanks unto Jehovah according to his righteousness, And will sing praise to the name of Jehovah Most High.

Psalm 8

For the Chief Musician; set to the Gittith. A Psalm of David.

1   O Jehovah, our Lord, How excellent is thy name in all the earth, Who hast set thy glory upon the heavens!

2   Out of the mouth of babes and sucklings hast thou established strength, Because of thine adversaries, That thou mightest still the enemy and the avenger.

3   When I consider thy heavens, the work of thy fingers, The moon and the stars, which thou hast ordained;

4   What is man, that thou art mindful of him? And the son of man, that thou visitest him?

5   For thou hast made him but little lower than God, And crownest him with glory and honor.

6   Thou makest him to have dominion over the works of thy hands; Thou hast put all things under his feet:

7   All sheep and oxen, Yea, and the beasts of the field,

8   The birds of the heavens, and the fish of the sea, Whatsoever passeth through the paths of the seas.

9   O Jehovah, our Lord, How excellent is thy name in all the earth!

Psalm 9

For the Chief Musician; set to Muthlabben. A Psalm of David.

1 I will give thanks unto Jehovah with my whole heart; I will show forth all thy marvellous works.

2 I will be glad and exult in thee; I will sing praise to thy name, O thou Most High.

3 When mine enemies turn back, They stumble and perish at thy presence.

4 For thou hast maintained my right and my cause; Thou sittest in the throne judging righteously.

5 Thou hast rebuked the nations, thou hast destroyed the wicked; Thou hast blotted out their name for ever and ever.

6 The enemy are come to an end, they are desolate for ever; And the cities which thou hast overthrown, The very remembrance of them is perished.

7 But Jehovah sitteth as king for ever: He hath prepared his throne for judgment;

8 And he will judge the world in righteousness, He will minister judgment to the peoples in uprightness.

9 Jehovah also will be a high tower for the oppressed, A high tower in times of trouble;

10 And they that know thy name will put their trust in thee; For thou, Jehovah, hast not forsaken them that seek thee.

11 Sing praises to Jehovah, who dwelleth in Zion: Declare among the people his doings.

12 For he that maketh inquisition for blood remembereth them; He forgetteth not the cry of the poor.

13 Have mercy upon me, O Jehovah; Behold my affliction which I suffer of them that hate me, Thou that liftest me up from the gates of death;

14 That I may show forth all thy praise. In the gates of the daughter of Zion I will rejoice in thy salvation.

15 The nations are sunk down in the pit that they made: In the net which they hid is their own foot taken.

16 Jehovah hath made himself known, he hath executed judgment: The wicked is snared in the work of his own hands. Higgaion. Selah

17 The wicked shall be turned back unto Sheol, Even all the nations that forget God.

18 For the needy shall not alway be forgotten, Nor the expectation of the poor perish for ever.

19 Arise, O Jehovah; let not man prevail: Let the nations be judged in thy sight.

20 Put them in fear, O Jehovah: Let the nations know themselves to be but men. Selah

Psalm 10

1   Why standest thou afar off, O Jehovah? Why hidest thou thyself in times of trouble?

2   In the pride of the wicked the poor is hotly pursued; Let them be taken in the devices that they have conceived.

3   For the wicked boasteth of his heart's desire, And the covetous renounceth, yea, contemneth Jehovah.

4   The wicked, in the pride of his countenance, saith, He will not require it. All his thoughts are, There is no God.

5   His ways are firm at all times; Thy judgments are far above out of his sight: As for all his adversaries, he puffeth at them.

6   He saith in his heart, I shall not be moved; To all generations I shall not be in adversity.

7   His mouth is full of cursing and deceit and oppression: Under his tongue is mischief and iniquity.

8   He sitteth in the lurking-places of the villages; In the secret places doth he murder the innocent; His eyes are privily set against the helpless.

9   He lurketh in secret as a lion in his covert; He lieth in wait to catch the poor: He doth catch the poor, when he draweth him in his net.

10   He croucheth, he boweth down, And the helpless fall by his strong ones.

11   He saith in his heart, God hath forgotten; He hideth his face; he will never see it.

12   Arise, O Jehovah; O God, lift up thy hand: Forget not the poor.

13   Wherefore doth the wicked contemn God, And say in his heart, Thou wilt not require it?

14   Thou hast seen it; for thou beholdest mischief and spite, to requite it with thy hand: The helpless committeth himself unto thee; Thou hast been the helper of the fatherless.

15   Break thou the arm of the wicked; And as for the evil man, seek out his wickedness till thou find none.

16   Jehovah is King for ever and ever: The nations are perished out of his land.

17   Jehovah, thou hast heard the desire of the meek: Thou wilt prepare their heart, thou wilt cause thine ear to hear;

18   To judge the fatherless and the oppressed, That man who is of the earth may be terrible no more.

Psalm 11

For the Chief Musician. A Psalm of David.

1   In Jehovah do I take refuge: How say ye to my soul, Flee as a bird to your mountain;

2   For, lo, the wicked bend the bow, They make ready their arrow upon the string, That they may shoot in darkness at the upright in heart;

3   If the foundations be destroyed, What can the righteous do?

4   Jehovah is in his holy temple; Jehovah, his throne is in heaven; His eyes behold, his eyelids try, the children of men.

5   Jehovah trieth the righteous; But the wicked and him that loveth violence his soul hateth.

6   Upon the wicked he will rain snares; Fire and brimstone and burning wind shall be the portion of their cup.

7   For Jehovah is righteous; he loveth righteousness: The upright shall behold his face.

Psalm 12

For the Chief Musician; set to the Sheminith. A Psalm of David.

1   Help, Jehovah; for the godly man ceaseth; For the faithful fail from among the children of men.

2   They speak falsehood every one with his neighbor: With flattering lip, and with a double heart, do they speak.

3   Jehovah will cut off all flattering lips, The tongue that speaketh great things;

4   Who have said, With our tongue will we prevail; Our lips are our own: who is lord over us?

5   Because of the oppression of the poor, because of the sighing of the needy, Now will I arise, saith Jehovah; I will set him in the safety he panteth for.

6   The words of Jehovah are pure words; As silver tried in a furnace on the earth, Purified seven times.

7   Thou wilt keep them, O Jehovah, Thou wilt preserve them from this generation for ever.

8   The wicked walk on every side, When vileness is exalted among the sons of men.

Psalm 13

For the Chief Musician. A Psalm of David.

1   How long, O Jehovah? wilt thou forget me for ever? How long wilt thou hide thy face from me?

2   How long shall I take counsel in my soul, Having sorrow in my heart all the day? How long shall mine enemy be exalted over me?

3   Consider and answer me, O Jehovah my God: Lighten mine eyes, lest I sleep the sleep of death;

4   Lest mine enemy say, I have prevailed against him; Lest mine adversaries rejoice when I am moved.

5   But I have trusted in thy lovingkindness; My heart shall rejoice in thy salvation.

6   I will sing unto Jehovah, Because he hath dealt bountifully with me.

Psalm 14

For the Chief Musician. A Psalm of David.

1 The fool hath said in his heart, There is no God. They are corrupt, they have done abominable works; There is none that doeth good.

2 Jehovah looked down from heaven upon the children of men, To see if there were any that did understand, That did seek after God.

3 They are all gone aside; they are together become filthy; There is none that doeth good, no, not one.

4 Have all the workers of iniquity no knowledge, Who eat up my people as they eat bread, And call not upon Jehovah?

5 There were they in great fear; For God is in the generation of the righteous.

6 Ye put to shame the counsel of the poor, Because Jehovah is his refuge.

7 Oh that the salvation of Israel were come out of Zion! When Jehovah bringeth back the captivity of his people, Then shall Jacob rejoice, and Israel shall be glad.

Psalm 15

A Psalm of David.

1   Jehovah, who shall sojourn in thy tabernacle? Who shall dwell in thy holy hill?

2   He that walketh uprightly, and worketh righteousness, And speaketh truth in his heart;

3   He that slandereth not with his tongue, Nor doeth evil to his friend, Nor taketh up a reproach against his neighbor;

4   In whose eyes a reprobate is despised, But who honoreth them that fear Jehovah; He that sweareth to his own hurt, and changeth not;

5   He that putteth not out his money to interest, Nor taketh reward against the innocent. He that doeth these things shall never be moved.

Psalm 16

Michtam of David.

¹ Preserve me, O God; for in thee do I take refuge.

² O my soul, thou hast said unto Jehovah, Thou art my Lord: I have no good beyond thee.

³ As for the saints that are in the earth, They are the excellent in whom is all my delight.

⁴ Their sorrows shall be multiplied that give gifts for another god: Their drink-offerings of blood will I not offer, Nor take their names upon my lips.

⁵ Jehovah is the portion of mine inheritance and of my cup: Thou maintainest my lot.

⁶ The lines are fallen unto me in pleasant places; Yea, I have a goodly heritage.

⁷ I will bless Jehovah, who hath given me counsel; Yea, my heart instructeth me in the night seasons.

⁸ I have set Jehovah always before me: Because he is at my right hand, I shall not be moved.

⁹ Therefore my heart is glad, and my glory rejoiceth; My flesh also shall dwell in safety.

¹⁰ For thou wilt not leave my soul to Sheol; Neither wilt thou suffer thy holy one to see corruption.

¹¹ Thou wilt show me the path of life: In thy presence is fulness of joy; In thy right hand there are pleasures for evermore.

Psalm 17

A Prayer of David.

1 Hear the right, O Jehovah, attend unto my cry; Give ear unto my prayer, that goeth not out of feigned lips.

2 Let my sentence come forth from thy presence; Let thine eyes look upon equity.

3 Thou hast proved my heart; thou hast visited me in the night; Thou hast tried me, and findest nothing; I am purposed that my mouth shall not transgress.

4 As for the works of men, by the word of thy lips I have kept me from the ways of the violent.

5 My steps have held fast to thy paths, My feet have not slipped.

6 I have called upon thee, for thou wilt answer me, O God: Incline thine ear unto me, and hear my speech.

7 Show thy marvellous lovingkindness, O thou that savest by thy right hand them that take refuge in thee From those that rise up against them.

8 Keep me as the apple of the eye; Hide me under the shadow of thy wings,

9 From the wicked that oppress me, My deadly enemies, that compass me about.

10 They are inclosed in their own fat: With their mouth they speak proudly.

11 They have now compassed us in our steps; They set their eyes to cast us down to the earth.

12   He is like a lion that is greedy of his prey, And as it were a young lion lurking in secret places.

13   Arise, O Jehovah, Confront him, cast him down: Deliver my soul from the wicked by thy sword;

14   From men by thy hand, O Jehovah, From men of the world, whose portion is in this life, And whose belly thou fillest with thy treasure: They are satisfied with children, And leave the rest of their substance to their babes.

15   As for me, I shall behold thy face in righteousness; I shall be satisfied, when I awake, with beholding thy form.

Psalm 18

For the Chief Musician. A Psalm of David the servant of Jehovah, who spake unto Jehovah the words of this song in the day that Jehovah delivered him from the hand of all his enemies, and from the hand of Saul: and he said,

1   I love thee, O Jehovah, my strength.

2   Jehovah is my rock, and my fortress, and my deliverer; My God, my rock, in whom I will take refuge; My shield, and the horn of my salvation, my high tower.

3   I will call upon Jehovah, who is worthy to be praised: So shall I be saved from mine enemies.

4   The cords of death compassed me, And the floods of ungodliness made me afraid.

5   The cords of Sheol were round about me; The snares of death came upon me.

6   In my distress I called upon Jehovah, And cried unto my God: He heard my voice out of his temple, And my cry before him came into his ears.

7   Then the earth shook and trembled; The foundations also of the mountains quaked And were shaken, because he was wroth.

8   There went up a smoke out of his nostrils, And fire out of his mouth devoured: Coals were kindled by it.

9   He bowed the heavens also, and came down; And thick darkness was under his feet.

10   And he rode upon a cherub, and did fly; Yea, he soared upon the wings of the wind.

11   He made darkness his hiding-place, his pavilion round about him, Darkness of waters, thick clouds of the skies.

12   At the brightness before him his thick clouds passed, Hailstones and coals of fire.

13   Jehovah also thundered in the heavens, And the Most High uttered his voice, Hailstones and coals of fire.

14   And he sent out his arrows, and scattered them; Yea, lightnings manifold, and discomfited them.

15   Then the channels of waters appeared, And the foundations of the world were laid bare, At thy rebuke, O Jehovah, At the blast of the breath of thy nostrils.

16   He sent from on high, he took me; He drew me out of many waters.

17   He delivered me from my strong enemy, And from them that hated me; for they were too mighty for me.

18   They came upon me in the day of my calamity; But Jehovah was my stay.

19   He brought me forth also into a large place; He delivered me, because he delighted in me.

20   Jehovah hath rewarded me according to my righteousness; According to the cleanness of my hands hath he recompensed me.

21   For I have kept the ways of Jehovah, And have not wickedly departed from my God.

22   For all his ordinances were before me, And I put not away his statutes from me.

23   I was also perfect with him, And I kept myself from mine iniquity.

24 Therefore hath Jehovah recompensed me according to my righteousness, According to the cleanness of my hands in his eyesight.

25 With the merciful thou wilt show thyself merciful; With the perfect man thou wilt show thyself perfect;

26 With the pure thou wilt show thyself pure; And with the perverse thou wilt show thyself froward.

27 For thou wilt save the afflicted people; But the haughty eyes thou wilt bring down.

28 For thou wilt light my lamp: Jehovah my God will lighten my darkness.

29 For by thee I run upon a troop; And by my God do I leap over a wall.

30 As for God, his way is perfect: The word of Jehovah is tried; He is a shield unto all them that take refuge in him.

31 For who is God, save Jehovah? And who is a rock, besides our God,

32 The God that girdeth me with strength, And maketh my way perfect?

33 He maketh my feet like hinds' feet: And setteth me upon my high places.

34 He teacheth my hands to war; So that mine arms do bend a bow of brass.

35 Thou hast also given me the shield of thy salvation; And thy right hand hath holden me up, And thy gentleness hath made me great.

36 Thou hast enlarged my steps under me, And my feet have not slipped.

37 I will pursue mine enemies, and overtake them; Neither will I turn again till they are consumed.

38   I will smite them through, so that they shall not be able to rise: They shall fall under my feet.

39   For thou hast girded me with strength unto the battle: Thou hast subdued under me those that rose up against me.

40   Thou hast also made mine enemies turn their backs unto me, That I might cut off them that hate me.

41   They cried, but there was none to save; Even unto Jehovah, but he answered them not.

42   Then did I beat them small as the dust before the wind; I did cast them out as the mire of the streets.

43   Thou hast delivered me from the strivings of the people; Thou hast made me the head of the nations: A people whom I have not known shall serve me.

44   As soon as they hear of me they shall obey me; The foreigners shall submit themselves unto me.

45   The foreigners shall fade away, And shall come trembling out of their close places.

46   Jehovah liveth; and blessed be my rock; And exalted be the God of my salvation,

47   Even the God that executeth vengeance for me, And subdueth peoples under me.

48   He rescueth me from mine enemies; Yea, thou liftest me up above them that rise up against me; Thou deliverest me from the violent man.

49   Therefore I will give thanks unto thee, O Jehovah, among the nations, And will sing praises unto thy name.

50   Great deliverance giveth he to his king, And showeth lovingkindness to his anointed, To David and to his seed, for evermore.

Psalm 19

For the Chief Musician. A Psalm of David.

1 The heavens declare the glory of God; And the firmament showeth his handiwork.

2 Day unto day uttereth speech, And night unto night showeth knowledge.

3 There is no speech nor language; Their voice is not heard.

4 Their line is gone out through all the earth, And their words to the end of the world. In them hath he set a tabernacle for the sun,

5 Which is as a bridegroom coming out of his chamber, And rejoiceth as a strong man to run his course.

6 His going forth is from the end of the heavens, And his circuit unto the ends of it; And there is nothing hid from the heat thereof.

7 The law of Jehovah is perfect, restoring the soul: The testimony of Jehovah is sure, making wise the simple.

8 The precepts of Jehovah are right, rejoicing the heart: The commandment of Jehovah is pure, enlightening the eyes.

9 The fear of Jehovah is clean, enduring for ever: The ordinances of Jehovah are true, and righteous altogether.

10 More to be desired are they than gold, yea, than much fine gold; Sweeter also than honey and the droppings of the honeycomb.

11 Moreover by them is thy servant warned: In keeping them there is great reward.

[12] Who can discern his errors? Clear thou me from hidden faults.

[13] Keep back thy servant also from presumptuous sins; Let them not have dominion over me: Then shall I be upright, And I shall be clear from great transgression.

[14] Let the words of my mouth and the meditation of my heart Be acceptable in thy sight, O Jehovah, my rock, and my redeemer.

Psalm 20

For the Chief Musician. A Psalm of David.

1   Jehovah answer thee in the day of trouble; The name of the God of Jacob set thee up on high;

2   Send thee help from the sanctuary, And strengthen thee out of Zion;

3   Remember all thy offerings, And accept thy burnt-sacrifice; Selah

4   Grant thee thy heart's desire, And fulfil all thy counsel.

5   We will triumph in thy salvation, And in the name of our God we will set up our banners: Jehovah fulfil all thy petitions.

6   Now know I that Jehovah saveth his anointed; He will answer him from his holy heaven With the saving strength of his right hand.

7   Some trust in chariots, and some in horses; But we will make mention of the name of Jehovah our God.

8   They are bowed down and fallen; But we are risen, and stand upright.

9   Save, Jehovah: Let the King answer us when we call.

Psalm 21

For the Chief Musician. A Psalm of David.

1   The king shall joy in thy strength, O Jehovah; And in thy salvation how greatly shall he rejoice!

2   Thou hast given him his heart's desire, And hast not withholden the request of his lips. Selah

3   For thou meetest him with the blessings of goodness: Thou settest a crown of fine gold on his head.

4   He asked life of thee, thou gavest it him, Even length of days for ever and ever.

5   His glory is great in thy salvation: Honor and majesty dost thou lay upon him.

6   For thou makest him most blessed for ever: Thou makest him glad with joy in thy presence.

7   For the king trusteth in Jehovah; And through the lovingkindness of the Most High he shall not be moved.

8   Thy hand will find out all thine enemies; Thy right hand will find out those that hate thee.

9   Thou wilt make them as a fiery furnace in the time of thine anger: Jehovah will swallow them up in his wrath, And the fire shall devour them.

10 Their fruit wilt thou destroy from the earth, And their seed from among the children of men.

11 For they intended evil against thee; They conceived a device which they are not able to perform.

12 For thou wilt make them turn their back; Thou wilt make ready with thy bowstrings against their face.

13 Be thou exalted, O Jehovah, in thy strength: So will we sing and praise thy power.

Psalm 22

For the Chief Musician; set to Aijaleth hash-Shahar. A Psalm of David.

1 My God, my God, why hast thou forsaken me? Why art thou so far from helping me, and from the words of my groaning?

2 O my God, I cry in the daytime, but thou answerest not; And in the night season, and am not silent.

3 But thou art holy, O thou that inhabitest the praises of Israel.

4 Our fathers trusted in thee: They trusted, and thou didst deliver them.

5 They cried unto thee, and were delivered: They trusted in thee, and were not put to shame.

6 But I am a worm, and no man; A reproach of men, and despised of the people.

7 All they that see me laugh me to scorn: They shoot out the lip, they shake the head, saying,

8 Commit thyself unto Jehovah; Let him deliver him: Let him rescue him, seeing he delighteth in him.

9 But thou art he that took me out of the womb; Thou didst make me trust when I was upon my mother's breasts.

10 I was cast upon thee from the womb; Thou art my God since my mother bare me.

11 Be not far from me; for trouble is near; For there is none to help.

12   Many bulls have compassed me; Strong bulls of Bashan have beset me round.

13   They gape upon me with their mouth, As a ravening and a roaring lion.

14   I am poured out like water, And all my bones are out of joint: My heart is like wax; It is melted within me.

15   My strength is dried up like a potsherd; And my tongue cleaveth to my jaws; And thou hast brought me into the dust of death.

16   For dogs have compassed me: A company of evil-doers have inclosed me; They pierced my hands and my feet.

17   I may count all my bones; They look and stare upon me.

18   They part my garments among them, And upon my vesture do they cast lots.

19   But be not thou far off, O Jehovah: O thou my succor, haste thee to help me.

20   Deliver my soul from the sword, My darling from the power of the dog.

21   Save me from the lion's mouth; Yea, from the horns of the wild-oxen thou hast answered me.

22   I will declare thy name unto my brethren: In the midst of the assembly will I praise thee.

23   Ye that fear Jehovah, praise him; All ye the seed of Jacob, glorify him; And stand in awe of him, all ye the seed of Israel.

24   For he hath not despised nor abhorred the affliction of the afflicted; Neither hath he hid his face from him; But when he cried unto him, he heard.

25   Of thee cometh my praise in the great assembly: I will pay my vows before them that fear him.

26   The meek shall eat and be satisfied; They shall praise Jehovah that seek after him: Let your heart live for ever.

27   All the ends of the earth shall remember and turn unto Jehovah; And all the kindreds of the nations shall worship before thee.

28   For the kingdom is Jehovah's; And he is the ruler over the nations.

29   All the fat ones of the earth shall eat and worship: All they that go down to the dust shall bow before him, Even he that cannot keep his soul alive.

30   A seed shall serve him; It shall be told of the Lord unto the next generation.

31   They shall come and shall declare his righteousness Unto a people that shall be born, that he hath done it.

Psalm 23

A Psalm of David.

1 Jehovah is my shepherd; I shall not want.

2 He maketh me to lie down in green pastures; He leadeth me beside still waters.

3 He restoreth my soul: He guideth me in the paths of righteousness for his name's sake.

4 Yea, thou I walk through the valley of the shadow of death, I will fear no evil; for thou art with me; Thy rod and thy staff, they comfort me.

5 Thou preparest a table before me in the presence of mine enemies: Thou hast anointed my head with oil; My cup runneth over.

6 Surely goodness and lovingkindness shall follow me all the days of my life; And I shall dwell in the house of Jehovah for ever.

Psalm 24

A Psalm of David.

¹ The earth is Jehovah's, and the fulness thereof; The world, and they that dwell therein.

² For he hath founded it upon the seas, And established it upon the floods.

³ Who shall ascend into the hill of Jehovah? And who shall stand in his holy place?

⁴ He that hath clean hands, and a pure heart; Who hath not lifted up his soul unto falsehood, And hath not sworn deceitfully.

⁵ He shall receive a blessing from Jehovah, And righteousness from the God of his salvation.

⁶ This is the generation of them that seek after him, That seek thy face, even Jacob. Selah

⁷ Lift up your heads, O ye gates; And be ye lifted up, ye everlasting doors: And the King of glory will come in.

⁸ Who is the King of glory? Jehovah strong and mighty, Jehovah mighty in battle.

⁹ Lift up your heads, O ye gates; Yea, lift them up, ye everlasting doors: And the King of glory will come in.

¹⁰ Who is this King of glory? Jehovah of hosts, He is the King of glory. Selah

Psalm 25

A Psalm of David.

1 Unto thee, O Jehovah, do I lift up my soul.

2 O my God, in thee have I trusted, Let me not be put to shame; Let not mine enemies triumph over me.

3 Yea, none that wait for thee shall be put to shame: They shall be put to shame that deal treacherously without cause.

4 Show me thy ways, O Jehovah; Teach me thy paths.

5 Guide me in thy truth, and teach me; For thou art the God of my salvation; For thee do I wait all the day.

6 Remember, O Jehovah, thy tender mercies and thy lovingkindness; For they have been ever of old.

7 Remember not the sins of my youth, nor my transgressions: According to thy lovingkindness remember thou me, For thy goodness' sake, O Jehovah.

8 Good and upright is Jehovah: Therefore will he instruct sinners in the way.

9 The meek will he guide in justice; And the meek will he teach his way.

10 All the paths of Jehovah are lovingkindness and truth Unto such as keep his covenant and his testimonies.

11 For thy name's sake, O Jehovah, Pardon mine iniquity, for it is great.

12 What man is he that feareth Jehovah? Him shall he instruct in the way that he shall choose.

13   His soul shall dwell at ease; And his seed shall inherit the land.

14   The friendship of Jehovah is with them that fear him; And he will show
      them his covenant.

15   Mine eyes are ever toward Jehovah; For he will pluck my feet out of the
      net.

16   Turn thee unto me, and have mercy upon me; For I am desolate and
      afflicted.

17   The troubles of my heart are enlarged: Oh bring thou me out of my
      distresses.

18   Consider mine affliction and my travail; And forgive all my sins.

19   Consider mine enemies, for they are many; And they hate me with cruel
      hatred.

20   Oh keep my soul, and deliver me: Let me not be put to shame, for I take
      refuge in thee.

21   Let integrity and uprightness preserve me, For I wait for thee.

22   Redeem Israel, O God, Out all of his troubles.

Psalm 26

A Psalm of David.

1 Judge me, O Jehovah, for I have walked in mine integrity: I have trusted also in Jehovah without wavering.

2 Examine me, O Jehovah, and prove me; Try my heart and my mind.

3 For thy lovingkindness is before mine eyes; And I have walked in thy truth.

4 I have not sat with men of falsehood; Neither will I go in with dissemblers.

5 I hate the assembly of evil-doers, And will not sit with the wicked.

6 I will wash my hands in innocency: So will I compass thine altar, O Jehovah;

7 That I may make the voice of thanksgiving to be heard, And tell of all thy wondrous works.

8 Jehovah, I love the habitation of thy house, And the place where thy glory dwelleth.

9 Gather not my soul with sinners, Nor my life with men of blood;

10 In whose hands is wickedness, And their right hand is full of bribes.

11 But as for me, I will walk in mine integrity: Redeem me, and be merciful unto me.

12 My foot standeth in an even place: In the congregations will I bless Jehovah.

Psalm 27

A Psalm of David.

1 Jehovah is my light and my salvation; Whom shall I fear? Jehovah is the strength of my life; Of whom shall I be afraid?

2 When evil-doers came upon me to eat up my flesh, Even mine adversaries and my foes, they stumbled and fell.

3 Though a host should encamp against me, My heart shall not fear: Though war should rise against me, Even then will I be confident.

4 One thing have I asked of Jehovah, that will I seek after; That I may dwell in the house of Jehovah all the days of my life, To behold the beauty of Jehovah, And to inquire in his temple.

5 For in the day of trouble he will keep me secretly in his pavilion: In the covert of his tabernacle will he hide me; He will lift me up upon a rock.

6 And now shall my head be lifted up above mine enemies round about me. And I will offer in his tabernacle sacrifices of joy; I will sing, yea, I will sing praises unto Jehovah.

7 Hear, O Jehovah, when I cry with my voice: Have mercy also upon me, and answer me.

8 When thou saidst, Seek ye my face; My heart said unto thee, Thy face, Jehovah, will I seek.

9 Hide not thy face from me; Put not thy servant away in anger: Thou hast been my help; Cast me not off, neither forsake me, O God of my salvation.

10   When my father and my mother forsake me, Then Jehovah will take me up.

11   Teach me thy way, O Jehovah; And lead me in a plain path, Because of mine enemies.

12   Deliver me not over unto the will of mine adversaries: For false witnesses are risen up against me, And such as breathe out cruelty.

13   I had fainted, unless I had believed to see the goodness of Jehovah In the land of the living.

14   Wait for Jehovah: Be strong, and let thy heart take courage; Yea, wait thou for Jehovah.

Psalm 28

A Psalm of David.

1 Unto thee, O Jehovah, will I call: My rock, be not thou deaf unto me; Lest, if thou be silent unto me, I become like them that go down into the pit.

2 Hear the voice of my supplications, when I cry unto thee, When I lift up my hands toward thy holy oracle.

3 Draw me not away with the wicked, And with the workers of iniquity; That speak peace with their neighbors, But mischief is in their hearts.

4 Give them according to their work, and according to the wickedness of their doings: Give them after the operation of their hands; Render to them their desert.

5 Because they regard not the works of Jehovah, Nor the operation of his hands, He will break them down and not build them up.

6 Blessed be Jehovah, Because he hath heard the voice of my supplications.

7 Jehovah is my strength and my shield; My heart hath trusted in him, and I am helped: Therefore my heart greatly rejoiceth; And with my song will I praise him.

8 Jehovah is their strength, And he is a stronghold of salvation to his anointed.

9 Save thy people, and bless thine inheritance: Be their shepherd also, and bear them up for ever.

Psalm 29

A Psalm of David.

1   Ascribe unto Jehovah, O ye sons of the mighty, Ascribe unto Jehovah glory and strength.

2   Ascribe unto Jehovah the glory due unto his name; Worship Jehovah in holy array.

3   The voice of Jehovah is upon the waters: The God of glory thundereth, Even Jehovah upon many waters.

4   The voice of Jehovah is powerful; The voice of Jehovah is full of majesty.

5   The voice of Jehovah breaketh the cedars; Yea, Jehovah breaketh in pieces the cedars of Lebanon.

6   He maketh them also to skip like a calf; Lebanon and Sirion like a young wild-ox.

7   The voice of Jehovah cleaveth the flames of fire.

8   The voice of Jehovah shaketh the wilderness; Jehovah shaketh the wilderness of Kadesh.

9   The voice of Jehovah maketh the hinds to calve, And strippeth the forests bare: And in his temple everything saith, Glory.

10 Jehovah sat as King at the Flood; Yea, Jehovah sitteth as King for ever.

11 Jehovah will give strength unto his people; Jehovah will bless his people with peace.

Psalm 30

A Psalm; a Song at the Dedication of the House. A Psalm of David.

1   I will extol thee, O Jehovah; for thou hast raised me up, And hast not made my foes to rejoice over me.

2   O Jehovah my God, I cried unto thee, and thou hast healed me.

3   O Jehovah, thou hast brought up my soul from Sheol; Thou hast kept me alive, that I should not go down to the pit.

4   Sing praise unto Jehovah, O ye saints of his, And give thanks to his holy memorial name.

5   For his anger is but for a moment; His favor is for a life-time: Weeping may tarry for the night, But joy cometh in the morning.

6   As for me, I said in my prosperity, I shall never be moved.

7   Thou, Jehovah, of thy favor hadst made my mountain to stand strong: Thou didst hide thy face; I was troubled.

8   I cried to thee, O Jehovah; And unto Jehovah I made supplication:

9   What profit is there in my blood, when I go down to the pit? Shall the dust praise thee? shall it declare thy truth?

10   Hear, O Jehovah, and have mercy upon me: Jehovah, be thou my helper.

11   Thou hast turned for me my mourning into dancing; Thou hast loosed my sackcloth, and girded me with gladness;

12   To the end that my glory may sing praise to thee, and not be silent. O Jehovah my God, I will give thanks unto thee for ever.

Psalm 31

For the Chief Musician. A Psalm of David.

1   In thee, O Jehovah, do I take refuge; Let me never be put to shame: Deliver me in thy righteousness.

2   Bow down thine ear unto me; deliver me speedily: Be thou to me a strong rock, A house of defence to save me.

3   For thou art my rock and my fortress; Therefore for thy name's sake lead me and guide me.

4   Pluck me out of the net that they have laid privily for me; For thou art my stronghold.

5   Into thy hand I commend my spirit: Thou hast redeemed me, O Jehovah, thou God of truth.

6   I hate them that regard lying vanities; But I trust in Jehovah.

7   I will be glad and rejoice in thy lovingkindness; For thou hast seen my affliction: Thou hast known my soul in adversities;

8   And thou hast not shut me up into the hand of the enemy; Thou hast set my feet in a large place.

9   Have mercy upon me, O Jehovah, for I am in distress: Mine eye wasteth away with grief, yea, my soul and my body.

10   For my life is spent with sorrow, And my years with sighing: My strength faileth because of mine iniquity, And my bones are wasted away.

11   Because of all mine adversaries I am become a reproach, Yea, unto my neighbors exceedingly, And a fear to mine acquaintance: They that did see me without fled from me.

12   I am forgotten as a dead man out of mind: I am like a broken vessel.

13   For I have heard the defaming of many, Terror on every side: While they took counsel together against me, They devised to take away my life.

14   But I trusted in thee, O Jehovah: I said, Thou art my God.

15   My times are in thy hand: Deliver me from the hand of mine enemies, and from them that persecute me.

16   Make thy face to shine upon thy servant: Save me in thy lovingkindness.

17   Let me not be put to shame, O Jehovah; for I have called upon thee: Let the wicked be put to shame, let them be silent in Sheol.

18   Let the lying lips be dumb, Which speak against the righteous insolently, With pride and contempt.

19   Oh how great is thy goodness, Which thou hast laid up for them that fear thee, Which thou hast wrought for them that take refuge in thee, Before the sons of men!

20   In the covert of thy presence wilt thou hide them from the plottings of man: Thou wilt keep them secretly in a pavilion from the strife of tongues.

21   Blessed be Jehovah; For he hath showed me his marvellous lovingkindness in a strong city.

22   As for me, I said in my haste, I am cut off from before thine eyes: Nevertheless thou heardest the voice of my supplications When I cried unto thee.

23   Oh love Jehovah, all ye his saints: Jehovah preserveth the faithful, And plentifully rewardeth him that dealeth proudly.

24   Be strong, and let your heart take courage, All ye that hope in Jehovah.

Psalm 32

A Psalm of David. Maschil.

1   Blessed is he whose transgression is forgiven, Whose sin is covered.

2   Blessed is the man unto whom Jehovah imputeth not iniquity, And in whose spirit there is no guile.

3   When I kept silence, my bones wasted away Through my groaning all the day long.

4   For day and night thy hand was heavy upon me: My moisture was changed as with the drought of summer. Selah

5   I acknowledged my sin unto thee, And mine iniquity did I not hide: I said, I will confess my transgressions unto Jehovah; And thou forgavest the iniquity of my sin. Selah

6   For this let every one that is godly pray unto thee in a time when thou mayest be found: Surely when the great waters overflow they shall not reach unto him.

7   Thou art my hiding-place; thou wilt preserve me from trouble; Thou wilt compass me about with songs of deliverance. Selah

8   I will instruct thee and teach thee in the way which thou shalt go: I will counsel thee with mine eye upon thee.

9   Be ye not as the horse, or as the mule, which have no understanding; Whose trappings must be bit and bridle to hold them in, Else they will not come near unto thee.

10   Many sorrows shall be to the wicked; But he that trusteth in Jehovah, lovingkindness shall compass him about.

11   Be glad in Jehovah, and rejoice, ye righteous; And shout for joy, all ye that are upright in heart.

Psalm 33

1   Rejoice in Jehovah, O ye righteous: Praise is comely for the upright.

2   Give thanks unto Jehovah with the harp: Sing praises unto him with the psaltery of ten strings.

3   Sing unto him a new song; Play skilfully with a loud noise.

4   For the word of Jehovah is right; And all his work is done in faithfulness.

5   He loveth righteousness and justice: The earth is full of the lovingkindness of Jehovah.

6   By the word of Jehovah were the heavens made, And all the host of them by the breath of his mouth.

7   He gathereth the waters of the sea together as a heap: He layeth up the deeps in store-houses.

8   Let all the earth fear Jehovah: Let all the inhabitants of the world stand in awe of him.

9   For he spake, and it was done; He commanded, and it stood fast.

10   Jehovah bringeth the counsel of the nations to nought; He maketh the thoughts of the peoples to be of no effect.

11   The counsel of Jehovah standeth fast for ever, The thoughts of his heart to all generations.

12   Blessed is the nation whose God is Jehovah, The people whom he hath chosen for his own inheritance.

13   Jehovah looketh from heaven; He beholdeth all the sons of men;

14 From the place of his habitation he looketh forth Upon all the inhabitants of the earth,

15 He that fashioneth the hearts of them all, That considereth all their works.

16 There is no king saved by the multitude of a host: A mighty man is not delivered by great strength.

17 A horse is a vain thing for safety; Neither doth he deliver any by his great power.

18 Behold, the eye of Jehovah is upon them that fear him, Upon them that hope in his lovingkindness;

19 To deliver their soul from death, And to keep them alive in famine.

20 Our soul hath waited for Jehovah: He is our help and our shield.

21 For our heart shall rejoice in him, Because we have trusted in his holy name.

22 Let thy loving kindness, O Jehovah, be upon us, According as we have hoped in thee.

Psalm 34

A Psalm of David; when he changed his behavior before Abimelech, who drove him away, and he departed.

1   I will bless Jehovah at all times: His praise shall continually be in my mouth.

2   My soul shall make her boast in Jehovah: The meek shall hear thereof, and be glad.

3   Oh magnify Jehovah with me, And let us exalt his name together.

4   I sought Jehovah, and he answered me, And delivered me from all my fears.

5   They looked unto him, and were radiant; And their faces shall never be confounded.

6   This poor man cried, and Jehovah heard him, And saved him out of all his troubles.

7   The angel of Jehovah encampeth round about them that fear him, And delivereth them.

8   Oh taste and see that Jehovah is good: Blessed is the man that taketh refuge in him.

9   Oh fear Jehovah, ye his saints; For there is no want to them that fear him.

10 The young lions do lack, and suffer hunger; But they that seek Jehovah shall not want any good thing.

11 Come, ye children, hearken unto me: I will teach you the fear of Jehovah.

¹² What man is he that desireth life, And loveth many days, that he may see good?

¹³ Keep thy tongue from evil, And thy lips from speaking guile.

¹⁴ Depart from evil, and do good; Seek peace, and pursue it.

¹⁵ The eyes of Jehovah are toward the righteous, And his ears are open unto their cry.

¹⁶ The face of Jehovah is against them that do evil, To cut off the remembrance of them from the earth.

¹⁷ The righteous cried, and Jehovah heard, And delivered them out of all their troubles.

¹⁸ Jehovah is nigh unto them that are of a broken heart, And saveth such as are of a contrite spirit.

¹⁹ Many are the afflictions of the righteous; But Jehovah delivereth him out of them all.

²⁰ He keepeth all his bones: Not one of them is broken.

²¹ Evil shall slay the wicked; And they that hate the righteous shall be condemned.

²² Jehovah redeemeth the soul of his servants; And none of them that take refuge in him shall be condemned.

Psalm 35

A Psalm of David.

1　Strive thou, O Jehovah, with them that strive with me: Fight thou against them that fight against me.

2　Take hold of shield and buckler, And stand up for my help.

3　Draw out also the spear, and stop the way against them that pursue me: Say unto my soul, I am thy salvation.

4　Let them be put to shame and brought to dishonor that seek after my soul: Let them be turned back and confounded that devise my hurt.

5　Let them be as chaff before the wind, And the angel of Jehovah driving them on.

6　Let their way be dark and slippery, And the angel of Jehovah pursuing them.

7　For without cause have they hid for me their net in a pit; Without cause have they digged a pit for my soul.

8　Let destruction come upon him unawares; And let his net that he hath hid catch himself: With destruction let him fall therein.

9　And my soul shall be joyful in Jehovah: It shall rejoice in his salvation.

10　All my bones shall say, Jehovah, who is like unto thee, Who deliverest the poor from him that is too strong for him, Yea, the poor and the needy from him that robbeth him?

11　Unrighteous witnesses rise up; They ask me of things that I know not.

12　They reward me evil for good, To the bereaving of my soul.

13 But as for me, when they were sick, my clothing was sackcloth: I afflicted my soul with fasting; And my prayer returned into mine own bosom.

14 I behaved myself as though it had been my friend or my brother: I bowed down mourning, as one that bewaileth his mother.

15 But in mine adversity they rejoiced, and gathered themselves together: The abjects gathered themselves together against me, and I knew it not; They did tear me, and ceased not:

16 Like the profane mockers in feasts, They gnashed upon me with their teeth.

17 Lord, how long wilt thou look on? Rescue my soul from their destructions, My darling from the lions.

18 I will give thee thanks in the great assembly: I will praise thee among much people.

19 Let not them that are mine enemies wrongfully rejoice over me; Neither let them wink with the eye that hate me without a cause.

20 For they speak not peace; But they devise deceitful words against them that are quiet in the land.

21 Yea, they opened their mouth wide against me; They said, Aha, aha, our eye hath seen it.

22 Thou hast seen it, O Jehovah; keep not silence: O Lord, be not far from me.

23 Stir up thyself, and awake to the justice due unto me, Even unto my cause, my God and my Lord.

24 Judge me, O Jehovah my God, according to thy righteousness; And let them not rejoice over me.

25 Let them not say in their heart, Aha, so would we have it: Let them not say, We have swallowed him up.

[26] Let them be put to shame and confounded together that rejoice at my hurt: Let them be clothed with shame and dishonor that magnify themselves against me.

[27] Let them shout for joy, and be glad, that favor my righteous cause: Yea, let them say continually, Jehovah be magnified, Who hath pleasure in the prosperity of his servant.

[28] And my tongue shall talk of thy righteousness And of thy praise all the day long.

Psalm 36

For the Chief Musician. A Psalm of David the servant of Jehovah.

1. The transgression of the wicked saith within my heart, There is no fear of God before his eyes.

2. For he flattereth himself in his own eyes, That his iniquity will not be found out and be hated.

3. The words of his mouth are iniquity and deceit: He hath ceased to be wise and to do good.

4. He deviseth iniquity upon his bed; He setteth himself in a way that is not good; He abhorreth not evil.

5. Thy lovingkindness, O Jehovah, is in the heavens; Thy faithfulness reacheth unto the skies.

6. Thy righteousness is like the mountains of God; Thy judgments are a great deep: O Jehovah, thou preservest man and beast.

7. How precious is thy lovingkindness, O God! And the children of men take refuge under the shadow of thy wings.

8. They shall be abundantly satisfied with the fatness of thy house; And thou wilt make them drink of the river of thy pleasures.

9. For with thee is the fountain of life: In thy light shall we see light.

10. Oh continue thy lovingkindness unto them that know thee, And thy righteousness to the upright in heart.

11. Let not the foot of pride come against me, And let not the hand of the wicked drive me away.

12. There are the workers of iniquity fallen: They are thrust down, and shall not be able to rise.

Psalm 37

A Psalm of David.

1   Fret not thyself because of evil-doers, Neither be thou envious against them that work unrighteousness.

2   For they shall soon be cut down like the grass, And wither as the green herb.

3   Trust in Jehovah, and do good; Dwell in the land, and feed on his faithfulness.

4   Delight thyself also in Jehovah; And he will give thee the desires of thy heart.

5   Commit thy way unto Jehovah; Trust also in him, and he will bring it to pass.

6   And he will make thy righteousness to go forth as the light, And thy justice as the noon-day.

7   Rest in Jehovah, and wait patiently for him: Fret not thyself because of him who prospereth in his way, Because of the man who bringeth wicked devices to pass.

8   Cease from anger, and forsake wrath: Fret not thyself, it tendeth only to evil-doing.

9   For evil-doers shall be cut off; But those that wait for Jehovah, they shall inherit the land.

10   For yet a little while, and the wicked shall not be: Yea, thou shalt diligently consider his place, and he shall not be.

11 But the meek shall inherit the land, And shall delight themselves in the abundance of peace.

12 The wicked plotteth against the just, And gnasheth upon him with his teeth.

13 The Lord will laugh at him; For he seeth that his day is coming.

14 The wicked have drawn out the sword, and have bent their bow, To cast down the poor and needy, To slay such as are upright in the way.

15 Their sword shall enter into their own heart, And their bows shall be broken.

16 Better is a little that the righteous hath Than the abundance of many wicked.

17 For the arms of the wicked shall be broken; But Jehovah upholdeth the righteous.

18 Jehovah knoweth the days of the perfect; And their inheritance shall be for ever.

19 They shall not be put to shame in the time of evil; And in the days of famine they shall be satisfied.

20 But the wicked shall perish, And the enemies of Jehovah shall be as the fat of lambs: They shall consume; In smoke shall they consume away.

21 The wicked borroweth, and payeth not again; But the righteous dealeth graciously, and giveth.

22 For such as are blessed of him shall inherit the land; And they that are cursed of him shall be cut off.

23 A man's goings are established of Jehovah; And he delighteth in his way.

24 Though he fall, he shall not be utterly cast down; For Jehovah upholdeth him with his hand.

25 I have been young, and now am old; Yet have I not seen the righteous forsaken, Nor his seed begging bread.

26 All the day long he dealeth graciously, and lendeth; And his seed is blessed.

27 Depart from evil, and do good; And dwell for evermore.

28 For Jehovah loveth justice, And forsaketh not his saints; They are preserved for ever: But the seed of the wicked shall be cut off.

29 The righteous shall inherit the land, And dwell therein for ever.

30 The mouth of the righteous talketh of wisdom, And his tongue speaketh justice.

31 The law of his God is in his heart; None of his steps shall slide.

32 The wicked watcheth the righteous, And seeketh to slay him.

33 Jehovah will not leave him in his hand, Nor condemn him when he is judged.

34 Wait for Jehovah, and keep his way, And he will exalt thee to inherit the land: When the wicked are cut off, thou shalt see it.

35 I have seen the wicked in great power, And spreading himself like a green tree in its native soil.

36 But one passed by, and, lo, he was not: Yea, I sought him, but he could not be found.

37 Mark the perfect man, and behold the upright; For there is a happy end to the man of peace.

38 As for transgressors, they shall be destroyed together; The end of the wicked shall be cut off.

39 But the salvation of the righteous is of Jehovah; He is their stronghold in the time of trouble.

40 And Jehovah helpeth them, and rescueth them; He rescueth them from the wicked, and saveth them, Because they have taken refuge in him.

Psalm 38

A Psalm of David, to bring to remembrance.

1 O Jehovah, rebuke me not in thy wrath; Neither chasten me in thy hot displeasure.

2 For thine arrows stick fast in me, And thy hand presseth me sore.

3 There is no soundness in my flesh because of thine indignation; Neither is there any health in my bones because of my sin.

4 For mine iniquities are gone over my head: As a heavy burden they are too heavy for me.

5 My wounds are loathsome and corrupt, Because of my foolishness.

6 I am pained and bowed down greatly; I go mourning all the day long.

7 For my loins are filled with burning; And there is no soundness in my flesh.

8 I am faint and sore bruised: I have groaned by reason of the disquietness of my heart.

9 Lord, all my desire is before thee; And my groaning is not hid from thee.

10 My heart throbbeth, my strength faileth me: As for the light of mine eyes, it also is gone from me.

11 My lovers and my friends stand aloof from my plague; And my kinsmen stand afar off.

12 They also that seek after my life lay snares for me; And they that seek my hurt speak mischievous things, And meditate deceits all the day long.

13 But I, as a deaf man, hear not; And I am as a dumb man that openeth not his mouth.

14 Yea, I am as a man that heareth not, And in whose mouth are no reproofs.

15 For in thee, O Jehovah, do I hope: Thou wilt answer, O Lord my God.

16 For I said, Lest they rejoice over me: When my foot slippeth, they magnify themselves against me.

17 For I am ready to fall, And my sorrow is continually before me.

18 For I will declare mine iniquity; I will be sorry for my sin.

19 But mine enemies are lively, and are strong; And they that hate me wrongfully are multiplied.

20 They also that render evil for good Are adversaries unto me, because I follow the thing that is good.

21 Forsake me not, O Jehovah: O my God, be not far from me.

22 Make haste to help me, O Lord, my salvation.

Psalm 39

For the Chief Musician, Jeduthun. A Psalm of David.

1   I said, I will take heed to my ways, That I sin not with my tongue: I will keep my mouth with a bridle, While the wicked is before me.

2   I was dumb with silence, I held my peace, even from good; And my sorrow was stirred.

3   My heart was hot within me; While I was musing the fire burned: Then spake I with my tongue:

4   Jehovah, make me to know mine end, And the measure of my days, what it is; Let me know how frail I am.

5   Behold, thou hast made my days as handbreadths; And my life-time is as nothing before thee: Surely every man at his best estate is altogether vanity. Selah

6   Surely every man walketh in a vain show; Surely they are disquieted in vain: He heapeth up riches, and knoweth not who shall gather them.

7   And now, Lord, what wait I for? My hope is in thee.

8   Deliver me from all my transgressions: Make me not the reproach of the foolish.

9   I was dumb, I opened not my mouth; Because thou didst it.

10   Remove thy stroke away from me: I am consumed by the blow of thy hand.

11 When thou with rebukes dost correct man for iniquity, Thou makest his beauty to consume away like a moth: Surely every man is vanity. Selah

12 Hear my prayer, O Jehovah, and give ear unto my cry; Hold not thy peace at my tears: For I am a stranger with thee, A sojourner, as all my fathers were.

13 Oh spare me, that I may recover strength, Before I go hence, and be no more.

Psalm 40

For the Chief Musician. A Psalm of David.

1   I waited patiently for Jehovah; And he inclined unto me, and heard my cry.

2   He brought me up also out of a horrible pit, out of the miry clay; And he set my feet upon a rock, and established my goings.

3   And he hath put a new song in my mouth, even praise unto our God: Many shall see it, and fear, And shall trust in Jehovah.

4   Blessed is the man that maketh Jehovah his trust, And respecteth not the proud, nor such as turn aside to lies.

5   Many, O Jehovah my God, are the wonderful works which thou hast done, And thy thoughts which are to us-ward; They cannot be set in order unto thee; If I would declare and speak of them, They are more than can be numbered.

6   Sacrifice and offering thou hast no delight in; Mine ears hast thou opened: Burnt-offering and sin-offering hast thou not required.

7   Then said I, Lo, I am come; In the roll of the book it is written of me:

8   I delight to do thy will, O my God; Yea, thy law is within my heart.

9   I have proclaimed glad tidings of righteousness in the great assembly; Lo, I will not refrain my lips, O Jehovah, thou knowest.

10 I have not hid thy righteousness within my heart; I have declared thy faithfulness and thy salvation; I have not concealed thy lovingkindness and thy truth from the great assembly.

11 Withhold not thou thy tender mercies from me, O Jehovah; Let thy lovingkindness and thy truth continually preserve me.

12 For innumerable evils have compassed me about; Mine iniquities have overtaken me, so that I am not able to look up; They are more than the hairs of my head; And my heart hath failed me.

13 Be pleased, O Jehovah, to deliver me: Make haste to help me, O Jehovah.

14 Let them be put to shame and confounded together That seek after my soul to destroy it: Let them be turned backward and brought to dishonor That delight in my hurt.

15 Let them be desolate by reason of their shame That say unto me, Aha, aha.

16 Let all those that seek thee rejoice and be glad in thee: Let such as love thy salvation say continually, Jehovah be magnified.

17 But I am poor and needy; Yet the Lord thinketh upon me: Thou art my help and my deliverer; Make no tarrying, O my God.

Psalm 41

For the Chief Musician. A Psalm of David.

1   Blessed is he that considereth the poor: Jehovah will deliver him in the day of evil.

2   Jehovah will preserve him, and keep him alive, And he shall be blessed upon the earth; And deliver not thou him unto the will of his enemies.

3   Jehovah will support him upon the couch of languishing: Thou makest all his bed in his sickness.

4   I said, O Jehovah, have mercy upon me: Heal my soul; for I have sinned against thee.

5   Mine enemies speak evil against me, saying, When will he die, and his name perish?

6   And if he come to see me, he speaketh falsehood; His heart gathereth iniquity to itself: When he goeth abroad, he telleth it.

7   All that hate me whisper together against me; Against me do they devise my hurt.

8   An evil disease, say they, cleaveth fast unto him; And now that he lieth he shall rise up no more.

9   Yea, mine own familiar friend, in whom I trusted, Who did eat of my bread, Hath lifted up his heel against me.

10   But thou, O Jehovah, have mercy upon me, and raise me up, That I may requite them.

11 By this I know that thou delightest in me, Because mine enemy doth not triumph over me.

12 And as for me, thou upholdest me in mine integrity, And settest me before thy face for ever.

13 Blessed be Jehovah, the God of Israel, From everlasting and to everlasting. Amen, and Amen.

Psalm 42

For the Chief Musician. Maschil of the sons of Korah.

1   As the hart panteth after the water brooks, So panteth my soul after thee, O God.

2   My soul thirsteth for God, for the living God: When shall I come and appear before God?

3   My tears have been my food day and night, While they continually say unto me, Where is thy God?

4   These things I remember, and pour out my soul within me, How I went with the throng, and led them to the house of God, With the voice of joy and praise, a multitude keeping holyday.

5   Why art thou cast down, O my soul? And why art thou disquieted within me? Hope thou in God; for I shall yet praise him For the help of his countenance.

6   O my God, my soul is cast down within me: Therefore do I remember thee from the land of the Jordan, And the Hermons, from the hill Mizar.

7   Deep calleth unto deep at the noise of thy waterfalls: All thy waves and thy billows are gone over me.

8   Yet Jehovah will command his lovingkindness in the day-time; And in the night his song shall be with me, Even a prayer unto the God of my life.

9   I will say unto God my rock, Why hast thou forgotten me? Why go I mourning because of the oppression of the enemy?

10   As with a sword in my bones, mine adversaries reproach me, While they continually say unto me, Where is thy God?

11   Why art thou cast down, O my soul? And why art thou disquieted within me? Hope thou in God; for I shall yet praise him, Who is the help of my countenance, and my God.

Psalm 43

1　Judge me, O God, and plead my cause against an ungodly nation: Oh deliver me from the deceitful and unjust man.

2　For thou art the God of my strength; why hast thou cast me off? Why go I mourning because of the oppression of the enemy?

3　Oh send out thy light and thy truth; let them lead me: Let them bring me unto thy holy hill, And to thy tabernacles.

4　Then will I go unto the altar of God, Unto God my exceeding joy; And upon the harp will I praise thee, O God, my God.

5　Why art thou cast down, O my soul? And why art thou disquieted within me? Hope thou in God; for I shall yet praise him, Who is the help of my countenance, and my God.

Psalm 44

For the Chief Musician. A Psalm of the sons of Korah. Maschil.

1 We have heard with our ears, O God, Our fathers have told us, What work thou didst in their days, In the days of old.

2 Thou didst drive out the nations with thy hand; But them thou didst plant: Thou didst afflict the peoples; But them thou didst spread abroad.

3 For they gat not the land in possession by their own sword, Neither did their own arm save them; But thy right hand, and thine arm, and the light of thy countenance, Because thou wast favorable unto them.

4 Thou art my King, O God: Command deliverance for Jacob.

5 Through thee will we push down our adversaries: Through thy name will we tread them under that rise up against us.

6 For I will not trust in my bow, Neither shall my sword save me.

7 But thou hast saved us from our adversaries, And hast put them to shame that hate us.

8 In God have we made our boast all the day long, And we will give thanks unto thy name for ever. Selah

9 But now thou hast cast us off, and brought us to dishonor, And goest not forth with our hosts.

10 Thou makest us to turn back from the adversary; And they that hate us take spoil for themselves.

11 Thou hast made us like sheep appointed for food, And hast scattered us among the nations.

12 Thou sellest thy people for nought, And hast not increased thy wealth by their price.

13 Thou makest us a reproach to our neighbors, A scoffing and a derision to them that are round about us.

14 Thou makest us a byword among the nations, A shaking of the head among the peoples.

15 All the day long is my dishonor before me, And the shame of my face hath covered me,

16 For the voice of him that reproacheth and blasphemeth, By reason of the enemy and the avenger.

17 All this is come upon us; Yet have we not forgotten thee, Neither have we dealt falsely in thy covenant.

18 Our heart is not turned back, Neither have our steps declined from thy way,

19 That thou hast sore broken us in the place of jackals, And covered us with the shadow of death.

20 If we have forgotten the name of our God, Or spread forth our hands to a strange god;

21 Will not God search this out? For he knoweth the secrets of the heart.

22 Yea, for thy sake are we killed all the day long; We are accounted as sheep for the slaughter.

23 Awake, why sleepest thou, O Lord? Arise, cast us not off for ever.

24 Wherefore hidest thou thy face, And forgettest our affliction and our oppression?

25 For our soul is bowed down to the dust: Our body cleaveth unto the earth.

26 Rise up for our help, And redeem us for thy loving kindness' sake.

Psalm 45

For the Chief Musician; set to Shoshannim. A Psalm of the sons of Korah. Maschil. A Song of loves.

1 My heart overfloweth with a goodly matter; I speak the things which I have made touching the king: My tongue is the pen of a ready writer.

2 Thou art fairer than the children of men; Grace is poured into thy lips: Therefore God hath blessed thee for ever.

3 Gird thy sword upon thy thigh, O mighty one, Thy glory and thy majesty.

4 And in thy majesty ride on prosperously, Because of truth and meekness and righteousness: And thy right hand shall teach thee terrible things.

5 Thine arrows are sharp; The peoples fall under thee; They are in the heart of the king's enemies.

6 Thy throne, O God, is for ever and ever: A sceptre of equity is the sceptre of thy kingdom.

7 Thou hast loved righteousness, and hated wickedness: Therefore God, thy God, hath anointed thee With the oil of gladness above thy fellows.

8 All thy garments smell of myrrh, and aloes, and cassia; Out of ivory palaces stringed instruments have made thee glad.

9 Kings' daughters are among thy honorable women: At thy right hand doth stand the queen in gold of Ophir.

10 Hearken, O daughter, and consider, and incline thine ear; Forget also thine own people, and thy father's house:

11 So will the king desire thy beauty; For he is thy lord; and reverence thou him.

12 And the daughter of Tyre shall be there with a gift; The rich among the people shall entreat thy favor.

13 The king's daughter within the palace is all glorious: Her clothing is inwrought with gold.

14 She shall be led unto the king in broidered work: The virgins her companions that follow her Shall be brought unto thee.

15 With gladness and rejoicing shall they be led: They shall enter into the king's palace.

16 Instead of thy fathers shall be thy children, Whom thou shalt make princes in all the earth.

17 I will make thy name to be remembered in all generations: Therefore shall the peoples give thee thanks for ever and ever.

Psalm 46

For the Chief Musician. A Psalm of the sons of Korah; set to Alamoth. A Song.

1   God is our refuge and strength, A very present help in trouble.

2   Therefore will we not fear, though the earth do change, And though the mountains be shaken into the heart of the seas;

3   Though the waters thereof roar and be troubled, Though the mountains tremble with the swelling thereof. Selah

4   There is a river, the streams whereof make glad the city of God, The holy place of the tabernacles of the Most High.

5   God is in the midst of her; she shall not be moved: God will help her, and that right early.

6   The nations raged, the kingdoms were moved: He uttered his voice, the earth melted.

7   Jehovah of hosts is with us; The God of Jacob is our refuge. Selah

8   Come, behold the works of Jehovah, What desolations he hath made in the earth.

9   He maketh wars to cease unto the end of the earth; He breaketh the bow, and cutteth the spear in sunder; He burneth the chariots in the fire.

10 Be still, and know that I am God: I will be exalted among the nations, I will be exalted in the earth.

11 Jehovah of hosts is with us; The God of Jacob is our refuge. Selah

Psalm 47

For the Chief Musician. A Psalm of the sons of Korah.

1   Oh clap your hands, all ye peoples; Shout unto God with the voice of triumph.

2   For Jehovah Most High is terrible; He is a great King over all the earth.

3   He subdueth peoples under us, And nations under our feet.

4   He chooseth our inheritance for us, The glory of Jacob whom he loved. Selah

5   God is gone up with a shout, Jehovah with the sound of a trumpet.

6   Sing praise to God, sing praises: Sing praises unto our King, sing praises.

7   For God is the King of all the earth: Sing ye praises with understanding.

8   God reigneth over the nations: God sitteth upon his holy throne.

9   The princes of the peoples are gathered together To be the people of the God of Abraham: For the shields of the earth belong unto God; He is greatly exalted.

Psalm 48

A Song; a Psalm of the sons of Korah.

1 Great is Jehovah, and greatly to be praised, In the city of our God, in his holy mountain.

2 Beautiful in elevation, the joy of the whole earth, Is mount Zion, on the sides of the north, The city of the great King.

3 God hath made himself known in her palaces for a refuge.

4 For, lo, the kings assembled themselves, They passed by together.

5 They saw it, then were they amazed; They were dismayed, they hasted away.

6 Trembling took hold of them there, Pain, as of a woman in travail.

7 With the east wind Thou breakest the ships of Tarshish.

8 As we have heard, so have we seen In the city of Jehovah of hosts, in the city of our God: God will establish it for ever. Selah

9 We have thought on thy loving kindness, O God, In the midst of thy temple.

10 As is thy name, O God, So is thy praise unto the ends of the earth: Thy right hand is full of righteousness.

11 Let mount Zion be glad, Let the daughters of Judah rejoice, Because of thy judgments.

12 Walk about Zion, and go round about her; Number the towers thereof;

13 Mark ye well her bulwarks; Consider her palaces: That ye may tell it to the generation following.

14 For this God is our God for ever and ever: He will be our guide even unto death.

Psalm 49

For the Chief Musician. A Psalm of the sons of Korah.

1   Hear this, all ye peoples; Give ear, all ye inhabitants of the world,

2   Both low and high, Rich and poor together.

3   My mouth shall speak wisdom; And the meditation of my heart shall be of understanding.

4   I will incline mine ear to a parable: I will open my dark saying upon the harp.

5   Wherefore should I fear in the days of evil, When iniquity at my heels compasseth me about?

6   They that trust in their wealth, And boast themselves in the multitude of their riches;

7   None of them can by any means redeem his brother, Nor give to God a ransom for him;

8   (For the redemption of their life is costly, And it faileth for ever;)

9   That he should still live alway, That he should not see corruption.

10   For he shall see it. Wise men die; The fool and the brutish alike perish, And leave their wealth to others.

11   Their inward thought is, that their houses shall continue for ever, And their dwelling-places to all generations; They call their lands after their own names.

12   But man being in honor abideth not: He is like the beasts that perish.

13 This their way is their folly: Yet after them men approve their sayings. Selah

14 They are appointed as a flock for Sheol; Death shall be their shepherd; And the upright shall have dominion over them in the morning; And their beauty shall be for Sheol to consume, That there be no habitation for it.

15 But God will redeem my soul from the power of Sheol; For he will receive me. Selah

16 Be not thou afraid when one is made rich, When the glory of his house is increased.

17 For when he dieth he shall carry nothing away; His glory shall not descend after him.

18 Though while he lived he blessed his soul (And men praise thee, when thou doest well to thyself,)

19 He shall go to the generation of his fathers; They shall never see the light.

20 Man that is in honor, and understandeth not, Is like the beasts that perish.

Psalm 50

A Psalm of Asaph.

1   The Mighty One, God, Jehovah, hath spoken, And called the earth from the rising of the sun unto the going down thereof.

2   Out of Zion, the perfection of beauty, God hath shined forth.

3   Our God cometh, and doth not keep silence: A fire devoureth before him, And it is very tempestuous round about him.

4   He calleth to the heavens above, And to the earth, that he may judge his people:

5   Gather my saints together unto me, Those that have made a covenant with me by sacrifice.

6   And the heavens shall declare his righteousness; For God is judge himself. Selah

7   Hear, O my people, and I will speak; O Israel, and I will testify unto thee: I am God, even thy God.

8   I will not reprove thee for thy sacrifices; And thy burnt-offerings are continually before me.

9   I will take no bullock out of thy house, Nor he-goats out of thy folds.

10   For every beast of the forest is mine, And the cattle upon a thousand hills.

11   I know all the birds of the mountains; And the wild beasts of the field are mine.

12   If I were hungry, I would not tell thee; For the world is mine, and the fulness thereof.

13   Will I eat the flesh of bulls, Or drink the blood of goats?

14   Offer unto God the sacrifice of thanksgiving; And pay thy vows unto the Most High:

15   And call upon me in the day of trouble; I will deliver thee, and thou shalt glorify me.

16   But unto the wicked God saith, What hast thou to do to declare my statutes, And that thou hast taken my covenant in thy mouth,

17   Seeing thou hatest instruction, And castest my words behind thee?

18   When thou sawest a thief, thou consentedst with him, And hast been partaker with adulterers.

19   Thou givest thy mouth to evil, And thy tongue frameth deceit.

20   Thou sittest and speakest against thy brother; Thou slanderest thine own mother's son.

21   These things hast thou done, and I kept silence; Thou thoughtest that I was altogether such a one as thyself: But I will reprove thee, and set them in order before thine eyes.

22   Now consider this, ye that forget God, Lest I tear you in pieces, and there be none to deliver:

23   Whoso offereth the sacrifice of thanksgiving glorifieth me; And to him that ordereth his way aright Will I show the salvation of God.

Psalm 51

For the Chief Musician. A Psalm of David; when Nathan the prophet came unto him, after he had gone in to Bathsheba.

1. Have mercy upon me, O God, according to thy lovingkindness: According to the multitude of thy tender mercies blot out my transgressions.

2. Wash me thoroughly from mine iniquity, And cleanse me from my sin.

3. For I know my transgressions; And my sin is ever before me.

4. Against thee, thee only, have I sinned, And done that which is evil in thy sight; That thou mayest be justified when thou speakest, And be clear when thou judgest.

5. Behold, I was brought forth in iniquity; And in sin did my mother conceive me.

6. Behold, thou desirest truth in the inward parts; And in the hidden part thou wilt make me to know wisdom.

7. Purify me with hyssop, and I shall be clean: Wash me, and I shall be whiter than snow.

8. Make me to hear joy and gladness, That the bones which thou hast broken may rejoice.

9. Hide thy face from my sins, And blot out all mine iniquities.

10. Create in me a clean heart, O God; And renew a right spirit within me.

11. Cast me not away from thy presence; And take not thy holy Spirit from me.

12   Restore unto me the joy of thy salvation; And uphold me with a willing spirit.

13   Then will I teach transgressors thy ways; And sinners shall be converted unto thee.

14   Deliver me from bloodguiltiness, O God, thou God of my salvation; And my tongue shall sing aloud of thy righteousness.

15   O Lord, open thou my lips; And my mouth shall show forth thy praise.

16   For thou delightest not in sacrifice; else would I give it: Thou hast no pleasure in burnt-offering.

17   The sacrifices of God are a broken spirit: A broken and contrite heart, O God, thou wilt not despise.

18   Do good in thy good pleasure unto Zion: Build thou the walls of Jerusalem.

19   Then will thou delight in the sacrifices of righteousness, In burnt-offering and in whole burnt-offering: Then will they offer bullocks upon thine altar.

Psalm 52

For the Chief Musician. Maschil of David; when Doeg the Edomite came and told Saul, and said unto him, David is come to the house of Abimelech.

1 Why boastest thou thyself in mischief, O mighty man? The lovingkindness of God endureth continually.

2 Thy tongue deviseth very wickedness, Like a sharp razor, working deceitfully.

3 Thou lovest evil more than good, And lying rather than to speak righteousness. Selah

4 Thou lovest all devouring words, thou deceitful tongue.

5 God will likewise destroy thee for ever; He will take thee up, and pluck thee out of thy tent, And root thee out of the land of the living. Selah

6 The righteous also shall see it, and fear, And shall laugh at him, saying,

7 Lo, this is the man that made not God his strength, But trusted in the abundance of his riches, And strengthened himself in his wickedness.

8 But as for me, I am like a green olive-tree in the house of God: I trust in the lovingkindness of God for ever and ever.

9 I will give thee thanks for ever, because thou hast done it; And I will hope in thy name, for it is good, in the presence of thy saints.

Psalm 53

For the Chief Musician; set to Mahalath. Maschil of David.

1 The fool hath said in his heart, There is no God. Corrupt are they, and have done abominable iniquity; There is none that doeth good.

2 God looked down from heaven upon the children of men, To see if there were any that did understand, That did seek after God.

3 Every one of them is gone back; they are together become filthy; There is none that doeth good, no, not one.

4 Have the workers of iniquity no knowledge, Who eat up my people as they eat bread, And call not upon God?

5 There were they in great fear, where no fear was; For God hath scattered the bones of him that encampeth against thee: Thou hast put them to shame, because of God hath rejected them.

6 Oh that the salvation of Israel were come out of Zion! When God bringeth back the captivity of his people, Then shall Jacob rejoice, and Israel shall be glad.

Psalm 54

For the Chief Musician; on stringed instruments. Maschil of David; when the Ziphites came and said to Saul, Doth not David hide himself with us?

1 Save me, O God, by thy name, And judge me in thy might.

2 Hear my prayer, O God; Give ear to the words of my mouth.

3 For strangers are risen up against me, And violent men have sought after my soul: They have not set God before them. Selah

4 Behold, God is my helper: The Lord is of them that uphold my soul.

5 He will requite the evil unto mine enemies: Destroy thou them in thy truth.

6 With a freewill-offering will I sacrifice unto thee: I will give thanks unto thy name, O Jehovah, for it is good.

7 For he hath delivered me out of all trouble; And mine eye hath seen my desire upon mine enemies.

Psalm 55

For the Chief Musician; on stringed instruments. Maschil of David.

¹ Give ear to my prayer, O God; And hide not thyself from my supplication.

² Attend unto me, and answer me: I am restless in my complaint, and moan,

³ Because of the voice of the enemy, Because of the oppression of the wicked; For they cast iniquity upon me, And in anger they persecute me.

⁴ My heart is sore pained within me: And the terrors of death are fallen upon me.

⁵ Fearfulness and trembling are come upon me, And horror hath overwhelmed me.

⁶ And I said, Oh that I had wings like a dove! Then would I fly away, and be at rest.

⁷ Lo, then would I wander far off, I would lodge in the wilderness. Selah

⁸ I would haste me to a shelter From the stormy wind and tempest.

⁹ Destroy, O Lord, and divide their tongue; For I have seen violence and strife in the city.

¹⁰ Day and night they go about it upon the walls thereof: Iniquity also and mischief are in the midst of it.

¹¹ Wickedness is in the midst thereof: Oppression and guile depart not from its streets.

¹² For it was not an enemy that reproached me; Then I could have borne it: Neither was it he that hated me that did magnify himself against me; Then I would have hid myself from him:

13 But it was thou, a man mine equal, My companion, and my familiar friend.

14 We took sweet counsel together; We walked in the house of God with the throng.

15 Let death come suddenly upon them, Let them go down alive into Sheol; For wickedness is in their dwelling, in the midst of them.

16 As for me, I will call upon God; And Jehovah will save me.

17 Evening, and morning, and at noonday, will I complain, and moan; And he will hear my voice.

18 He hath redeemed my soul in peace from the battle that was against me; For they were many that strove with me.

19 God will hear, and answer them, Even he that abideth of old, Selah The men who have no changes, And who fear not God.

20 He hath put forth his hands against such as were at peace with him: He hath profaned his covenant.

21 His mouth was smooth as butter, But his heart was war: His words were softer than oil, Yet were they drawn swords.

22 Cast thy burden upon Jehovah, and he will sustain thee: He will never suffer the righteous to be moved.

23 But thou, O God, wilt bring them down into the pit of destruction: Bloodthirsty and deceitful men shall not live out half their days; But I will trust in thee.

Psalm 56

For the Chief Musician; set to Jonath elem rehokim. A Psalm of David. Michtam: when the Philistines took him in Gath.

1   Be merciful unto me, O God; for man would swallow me up: All the day long he fighting oppresseth me.

2   Mine enemies would swallow me up all the day long; For they are many that fight proudly against me.

3   What time I am afraid, I will put my trust in thee.

4   In God (I will praise his word), In God have I put my trust, I will not be afraid; What can flesh do unto me?

5   All the day long they wrest my words: All their thoughts are against me for evil.

6   They gather themselves together, they hide themselves, They mark my steps, Even as they have waited for my soul.

7   Shall they escape by iniquity? In anger cast down the peoples, O God.

8   Thou numberest my wanderings: Put thou my tears into thy bottle; Are they not in thy book?

9   Then shall mine enemies turn back in the day that I call: This I know, that God is for me.

10   In God (I will praise his word), In Jehovah (I will praise his word),

11   In God have I put my trust, I will not be afraid; What can man do unto me?

12   Thy vows are upon me, O God: I will render thank-offerings unto thee.

13   For thou hast delivered my soul from death: Hast thou not delivered my feet from falling, That I may walk before God In the light of the living?

Psalm 57

For the Chief Musician; set to Al-tash-heth. A Psalm of David. Michtam; when he fled from Saul, in the cave.

1   Be merciful unto me, O God, be merciful unto me; For my soul taketh refuge in thee: Yea, in the shadow of thy wings will I take refuge, Until these calamities be overpast.

2   I will cry unto God Most High, Unto God that performeth all things for me.

3   He will send from heaven, and save me, When he that would swallow me up reproacheth; Selah God will send forth his lovingkindness and his truth.

4   My soul is among lions; I lie among them that are set on fire, Even the sons of men, whose teeth are spears and arrows, And their tongue a sharp sword.

5   Be thou exalted, O God, above the heavens; Let thy glory be above all the earth.

6   They have prepared a net for my steps; My soul is bowed down: They have digged a pit before me; They are fallen into the midst thereof themselves. Selah

7   My heart is fixed, O God, my heart is fixed: I will sing, yea, I will sing praises.

8   Awake up, my glory; awake, psaltery and harp: I myself will awake right early.

9   I will give thanks unto thee, O Lord, among the peoples: I will sing praises unto thee among the nations.

10   For thy lovingkindness is great unto the heavens, And thy truth unto the skies.

11   Be thou exalted, O God, above the heavens; Let thy glory be above all the earth.

Psalm 58

For the Chief Musician; set to Al-tashheth. A Psalm of David Michtam.

1 Do ye indeed in silence speak righteousness? Do ye judge uprightly, O ye sons of men?

2 Nay, in heart ye work wickedness; Ye weigh out the violence of your hands in the earth.

3 The wicked are estranged from the womb: They go astray as soon as they are born, speaking lies.

4 Their poison is like the poison of a serpent: They are like the deaf adder that stoppeth her ear,

5 Which hearkeneth not to the voice of charmers, Charming never so wisely.

6 Break their teeth, O God, in their mouth: Break out the great teeth of the young lions, O Jehovah.

7 Let them melt away as water that runneth apace: When he aimeth his arrows, let them be as though they were cut off.

8 Let them be as a snail which melteth and passeth away, Like the untimely birth of a woman, that hath not seen the sun.

9 Before your pots can feel the thorns, He will take them away with a whirlwind, the green and the burning alike.

10 The righteous shall rejoice when he seeth the vengeance: He shall wash his feet in the blood of the wicked;

11 So that men shall say, Verily there is a reward for the righteous: Verily there is a God that judgeth in the earth.

Psalm 59

For the Chief Musician; set to Al-tashheth. A Psalm of David.
Michtam; when Saul sent, and they watched the house to kill him.

1 Deliver me from mine enemies, O my God: Set me on high from them that rise up against me.

2 Deliver me from the workers of iniquity, And save me from the bloodthirsty men.

3 For, lo, they lie in wait for my soul; The mighty gather themselves together against me: Not for my transgression, nor for my sin, O Jehovah.

4 They run and prepare themselves without my fault: Awake thou to help me, and behold.

5 Even thou, O Jehovah God of hosts, the God of Israel, Arise to visit all the nations: Be not merciful to any wicked transgressors. Selah

6 They return at evening, they howl like a dog, And go round about the city.

7 Behold, they belch out with their mouth; Swords are in their lips: For who, say they, doth hear?

8 But thou, O Jehovah, wilt laugh at them; Thou wilt have all the nations in derision.

9 Because of his strength I will give heed unto thee; For God is my high tower.

10 My God with his lovingkindness will meet me: God will let me see my desire upon mine enemies.

11   Slay them not, lest my people forget: Scatter them by thy power, and bring them down, O Lord our shield.

12   For the sin of their mouth, and the words of their lips, Let them even be taken in their pride, And for cursing and lying which they speak.

13   Consume them in wrath, consume them, so that they shall be no more: And let them know that God ruleth in Jacob, Unto the ends of the earth. Selah

14   And at evening let them return, let them howl like a dog, And go round about the city.

15   They shall wander up and down for food, And tarry all night if they be not satisfied.

16   But I will sing of thy strength; Yea, I will sing aloud of thy lovingkindness in the morning: For thou hast been my high tower, And a refuge in the day of my distress.

17   Unto thee, O my strength, will I sing praises: For God is my high tower, the God of my mercy.

Psalm 60

For the Chief Musician; set to Shushan Eduth. Michtam of David, to teach; and when he strove with Aram-naharaim and with Aram-zobah, and Joab returned, and smote of Edom in the Valley of Salt twelve thousand.

1. O God thou hast cast us off, thou hast broken us down; Thou hast been angry; oh restore us again.

2. Thou hast made the land to tremble; thou hast rent it: Heal the breaches thereof; for it shaketh.

3. Thou hast showed thy people hard things: Thou hast made us to drink the wine of staggering.

4. Thou hast given a banner to them that fear thee, That it may be displayed because of the truth. Selah

5. That thy beloved may be delivered, Save with thy right hand, and answer us.

6. God hath spoken in his holiness: I will exult; I will divide Shechem, and mete out the valley of Succoth.

7. Gilead is mine, and Manasseh is mine; Ephraim also is the defence of my head; Judah is my sceptre.

8. Moab is my washpot; Upon Edom will I cast my shoe: Philistia, shout thou because of me.

9. Who will bring me into the strong city? Who hath led me unto Edom?

¹⁰   Hast not thou, O God, cast us off? And thou goest not forth, O God, with our hosts.

¹¹   Give us help against the adversary; For vain is the help of man.

¹²   Through God we shall do valiantly; For he it is that will tread down our adversaries.

Psalm 61

For the Chief Musician; on a stringed instrument. A Psalm of David.

1 Hear my cry, O God; Attend unto my prayer.

2 From the end of the earth will I call unto thee, when my heart is overwhelmed: Lead me to the rock that is higher than I.

3 For thou hast been a refuge for me, A strong tower from the enemy.

4 I will dwell in thy tabernacle for ever: I will take refuge in the covert of thy wings. Selah

5 For thou, O God, hast heard my vows: Thou hast given me the heritage of those that fear thy name.

6 Thou wilt prolong the king's life; His years shall be as many generations.

7 He shall abide before God for ever: Oh prepare lovingkindness and truth, that they may preserve him.

8 So will I sing praise unto thy name for ever, That I may daily perform my vows.

Psalm 62

For the Chief Musician; after the manner of Jeduthan. A Psalm of David.

1   My soul waiteth in silence for God only: From him cometh my salvation.

2   He only is my rock and my salvation: He is my high tower; I shall not be greatly moved.

3   How long will ye set upon a man, That ye may slay him, all of you, Like a leaning wall, like a tottering fence?

4   They only consult to thrust him down from his dignity; They delight in lies; They bless with their mouth, but they curse inwardly. Selah

5   My soul, wait thou in silence for God only; For my expectation is from him.

6   He only is my rock and my salvation: He is my high tower; I shall not be moved.

7   With God is my salvation and my glory: The rock of my strength, and my refuge, is in God.

8   Trust in him at all times, ye people; Pour out your heart before him: God is a refuge for us. Selah

9   Surely men of low degree are vanity, and men of high degree are a lie: In the balances they will go up; They are together lighter than vanity.

10 Trust not in oppression, And become not vain in robbery: If riches increase, set not your heart thereon.

11 God hath spoken once, Twice have I heard this, That power belongeth unto God.

12 Also unto thee, O Lord, belongeth lovingkindness; For thou renderest to every man according to his work.

Psalm 63

A Psalm of David when he was in the wilderness of Judah.

1   O God, thou art my God; earnestly will I seek thee: My soul thirsteth for thee, my flesh longeth for thee, In a dry and weary land, where no water is.

2   So have I looked upon thee in the sanctuary, To see thy power and thy glory.

3   Because thy lovingkindness is better than life, My lips shall praise thee.

4   So will I bless thee while I live: I will lift up my hands in thy name.

5   My soul shall be satisfied as with marrow and fatness; And my mouth shall praise thee with joyful lips;

6   When I remember thee upon my bed, And meditate on thee in the night-watches.

7   For thou hast been my help, And in the shadow of thy wings will I rejoice.

8   My soul followeth hard after thee: Thy right hand upholdeth me.

9   But those that seek my soul, to destroy it, Shall go into the lower parts of the earth.

10   They shall be given over to the power of the sword: They shall be a portion for foxes.

11   But the king shall rejoice in God: Every one that sweareth by him shall glory; For the mouth of them that speak lies shall be stopped.

Psalm 64

For the Chief Musician. A Psalm of David.

1   Hear my voice, O God, in my complaint: Preserve my life from fear of the enemy.

2   Hide me from the secret counsel of evil-doers, From the tumult of the workers of iniquity;

3   Who have whet their tongue like a sword, And have aimed their arrows, even bitter words,

4   That they may shoot in secret places at the perfect: Suddenly do they shoot at him, and fear not.

5   They encourage themselves in an evil purpose; They commune of laying snares privily; They say, Who will see them?

6   They search out iniquities; We have accomplished, say they, a diligent search: And the inward thought and the heart of every one is deep.

7   But God will shoot at them; With an arrow suddenly shall they be wounded.

8   So they shall be made to stumble, their own tongue being against them: All that see them shall wag the head.

9   And all men shall fear; And they shall declare the work of God, And shall wisely consider of his doing.

10   The righteous shall be glad in Jehovah, and shall take refuge in him; And all the upright in heart shall glory.

Psalm 65

For the Chief Musician. A Psalm. A song of David.

1 Praise waiteth for thee, O God, in Zion; And unto thee shall the vow be performed.

2 O thou that hearest prayer, Unto thee shall all flesh come.

3 Iniquities prevail against me: As for our transgressions, thou wilt forgive them.

4 Blessed is the man whom thou choosest, and causest to approach unto thee, That he may dwell in thy courts: We shall be satisfied with the goodness of thy house, Thy holy temple.

5 By terrible things thou wilt answer us in righteousness, Oh God of our salvation, Thou that art the confidence of all the ends of the earth, And of them that are afar off upon the sea:

6 Who by his strength setteth fast the mountains, Being girded about with might;

7 Who stilleth the roaring of the seas, The roaring of their waves, And the tumult of the peoples.

8 They also that dwell in the uttermost parts are afraid at thy tokens: Thou makest the outgoings of the morning and evening to rejoice.

9 Thou visitest the earth, and waterest it, Thou greatly enrichest it; The river of God is full of water: Thou providest them grain, when thou hast so prepared the earth.

10 Thou waterest its furrows abundantly; Thou settlest the ridges thereof: Thou makest it soft with showers; Thou blessest the springing thereof.

11 Thou crownest the year with thy goodness; And thy paths drop fatness.

12 They drop upon the pastures of the wilderness; And the hills are girded with joy.

13 The pastures are clothed with flocks; The valleys also are covered over with grain; They shout for joy, they also sing.

Psalm 66

For the Chief Musician. A song, a Psalm.

1   Make a joyful noise unto God, all the earth:

2   Sing forth the glory of his name: Make his praise glorious.

3   Say unto God, How terrible are thy works! Through the greatness of thy power shall thine enemies submit themselves unto thee.

4   All the earth shall worship thee, And shall sing unto thee; They shall sing to thy name. Selah

5   Come, and see the works of God; He is terrible in his doing toward the children of men.

6   He turned the sea into dry land; They went through the river on foot: There did we rejoice in him.

7   He ruleth by his might for ever; His eyes observe the nations: Let not the rebellious exalt themselves. Selah

8   Oh bless our God, ye peoples, And make the voice of his praise to be heard;

9   Who holdeth our soul in life, And suffereth not our feet to be moved.

10   For thou, O God, hast proved us: Thou hast tried us, as silver is tried.

11   Thou broughtest us into the net; Thou layedst a sore burden upon our loins.

12   Thou didst cause men to ride over our heads; We went through fire and through water; But thou broughtest us out into a wealthy place.

13 I will come into thy house with burnt-offerings; I will pay thee my vows,

14 Which my lips uttered, And my mouth spake, when I was in distress.

15 I will offer unto thee burnt-offerings of fatlings, With the incense of rams; I will offer bullocks with goats. Selah

16 Come, and hear, all ye that fear God, And I will declare what he hath done for my soul.

17 I cried unto him with my mouth, And he was extolled with my tongue.

18 If I regard iniquity in my heart, The Lord will not hear:

19 But verily God hath heard; He hath attended to the voice of my prayer.

20 Blessed be God, Who hath not turned away my prayer, Nor his loving kindness from me.

Psalm 67

For the Chief Musician; on stringed instruments. A Psalm, a song.

1   God be merciful unto us, and bless us, And cause his face to shine upon us; Selah

2   That thy way may be known upon earth, Thy salvation among all nations.

3   Let the peoples praise thee, O God; Let all the peoples praise thee.

4   Oh let the nations be glad and sing for joy; For thou wilt judge the peoples with equity, And govern the nations upon earth. Selah

5   Let the peoples praise thee, O God; Let all the peoples praise thee.

6   The earth hath yielded its increase: God, even our own God, will bless us.

7   God will bless us; And all the ends of the earth shall fear him.

Psalm 68

For the Chief Musician; A Psalm of David, a song.

1 Let God arise, let his enemies be scattered; Let them also that hate him flee before him.

2 As smoke is driven away, so drive them away: As wax melteth before the fire, So let the wicked perish at the presence of God.

3 But let the righteous be glad; let them exult before God: Yea, let them rejoice with gladness.

4 Sing unto God, sing praises to his name: Cast up a highway for him that rideth through the deserts; His name is Jehovah; and exult ye before him.

5 A father of the fatherless, and a judge of the widows, Is God in his holy habitation.

6 God setteth the solitary in families: He bringeth out the prisoners into prosperity; But the rebellious dwell in a parched land.

7 O God, when thou wentest forth before thy people, When thou didst march through the wilderness; Selah

8 The earth trembled, The heavens also dropped rain at the presence of God: Yon Sinai trembled at the presence of God, the God of Israel.

9 Thou, O God, didst send a plentiful rain, Thou didst confirm thine inheritance, when it was weary.

10 Thy congregation dwelt therein: Thou, O God, didst prepare of thy goodness for the poor.

11 The Lord giveth the word: The women that publish the tidings are a great host.

12   Kings of armies flee, they flee; And she that tarrieth at home divideth the spoil.

13   When ye lie among the sheepfolds, It is as the wings of a dove covered with silver, And her pinions with yellow gold.

14   When the Almighty scattered kings therein, It was as when it snoweth in Zalmon.

15   A mountain of God is the mountain of Bashan; A high mountain is the mountain of Bashan.

16   Why look ye askance, ye high mountains, At the mountain which God hath desired for his abode? Yea, Jehovah will dwell in it for ever.

17   The chariots of God are twenty thousand, even thousands upon thousands; The Lord is among them, as in Sinai, in the sanctuary.

18   Thou hast ascended on high, thou hast led away captives; Thou hast received gifts among men, Yea, among the rebellious also, that Jehovah God might dwell with them.

19   Blessed be the Lord, who daily beareth our burden, Even the God who is our salvation. Selah

20   God is unto us a God of deliverances; And unto Jehovah the Lord belongeth escape from death.

21   But God will smite through the head of his enemies, The hairy scalp of such a one as goeth on still in his guiltiness.

22   The Lord said, I will bring again from Bashan, I will bring them again from the depths of the sea;

23   That thou mayest crush them, dipping thy foot in blood, That the tongue of thy dogs may have its portion from thine enemies.

24   They have seen thy goings, O God, Even the goings of my God, my King, into the sanctuary.

25 The singers went before, the minstrels followed after, In the midst of the damsels playing with timbrels.

26 Bless ye God in the congregations, Even the Lord, ye that are of the fountain of Israel.

27 There is little Benjamin their ruler, The princes of Judah and their council, The princes of Zebulun, the princes of Naphtali.

28 Thy God hath commanded thy strength: Strengthen, O God, that which thou hast wrought for us.

29 Because of thy temple at Jerusalem Kings shall bring presents unto thee.

30 Rebuke the wild beast of the reeds, The multitude of the bulls, with the calves of the peoples, Trampling under foot the pieces of silver: He hath scattered the peoples that delight in war.

31 Princes shall come out of Egypt; Ethiopia shall haste to stretch out her hands unto God.

32 Sing unto God, ye kingdoms of the earth; Oh sing praises unto the Lord; Selah

33 To him that rideth upon the heaven of heavens, which are of old; Lo, he uttereth his voice, a mighty voice.

34 Ascribe ye strength unto God: His excellency is over Israel, And his strength is in the skies.

35 O God, thou art terrible out of thy holy places: The God of Israel, he giveth strength and power unto his people. Blessed be God.

Psalm 69

For the Chief Musician; set to Shoshanim. A Psalm of David.

1 Save me, O God; For the waters are come in unto my soul.

2 I sink in deep mire, where there is no standing: I am come into deep waters, where the floods overflow me.

3 I am weary with my crying; my throat is dried: Mine eyes fail while I wait for my God.

4 They that hate me without a cause are more than the hairs of my head: They that would cut me off, being mine enemies wrongfully, are mighty: That which I took not away I have to restore.

5 O God, thou knowest my foolishness; And my sins are not hid from thee.

6 Let not them that wait for thee be put to shame through me, O Lord Jehovah of hosts: Let not those that seek thee be brought to dishonor through me, O God of Israel.

7 Because for thy sake I have borne reproach; Shame hath covered my face.

8 I am become a stranger unto my brethren, And an alien unto my mother's children.

9 For the zeal of thy house hath eaten me up; And the reproaches of them that reproach thee are fallen upon me.

10 When I wept, and chastened my soul with fasting, That was to my reproach.

11 When I made sackcloth my clothing, I became a byword unto them.

12 They that sit in the gate talk of me; And I am the song of the drunkards.

13 But as for me, my prayer is unto thee, O Jehovah, in an acceptable time: O God, in the abundance of thy lovingkindness, Answer me in the truth of thy salvation.

14 Deliver me out of the mire, and let me not sink: Let me be delivered from them that hate me, and out of the deep waters.

15 Let not the waterflood overwhelm me, Neither let the deep shallow me up; And let not the pit shut its mouth upon me.

16 Answer me, O Jehovah; for thy lovingkindness is good: According to the multitude of thy tender mercies turn thou unto me.

17 And hide not thy face from thy servant; For I am in distress; answer me speedily.

18 Draw nigh unto my soul, and redeem it: Ransom me because of mine enemies.

19 Thou knowest my reproach, and my shame, and my dishonor: Mine adversaries are all before thee.

20 Reproach hath broken my heart; and I am full of heaviness: And I looked for some to take pity, but there was none; And for comforters, but I found none.

21 They gave me also gall for my food; And in my thirst they gave me vinegar to drink.

22 Let their table before them become a snare; And when they are in peace, let it become a trap.

23 Let their eyes be darkened, so that they cannot see; And make their loins continually to shake.

24 Pour out thine indignation upon them, And let the fierceness of thine anger overtake them.

25   Let their habitation be desolate; Let none dwell in their tents.

26   For they persecute him whom thou hast smitten; And they tell of the sorrow of those whom thou hast wounded.

27   Add iniquity unto their iniquity; And let them not come into thy righteousness.

28   Let them be blotted out of the book of life, And not be written with the righteous.

29   But I am poor and sorrowful: Let thy salvation, O God, set me up on high.

30   I will praise the name of God with a song, And will magnify him with thanksgiving.

31   And it will please Jehovah better than an ox, Or a bullock that hath horns and hoofs.

32   The meek have seen it, and are glad: Ye that seek after God, let your heart live.

33   For Jehovah heareth the needy, And despiseth not his prisoners.

34   Let heaven and earth praise him, The seas, and everything that moveth therein.

35   For God will save Zion, and build the cities of Judah; And they shall abide there, and have it in possession.

36   The seed also of his servants shall inherit it; And they that love his name shall dwell therein.

Psalm 70

For the Chief Musician. A Psalm of David; to bring to remembrance.

1 Make haste, O God, to deliver me; Make haste to help me, O Jehovah.

2 Let them be put to shame and confounded That seek after my soul: Let them be turned backward and brought to dishonor That delight in my hurt.

3 Let them be turned back by reason of their shame That say, Aha, aha.

4 Let all those that seek thee rejoice and be glad in thee; And let such as love thy salvation say continually, Let God be magnified.

5 But I am poor and needy; Make haste unto me, O God: Thou art my help and my deliverer; O Jehovah, make no tarrying.

Psalm 71

1   In thee, O Jehovah, do I take refuge: Let me never be put to shame.

2   Deliver me in thy righteousness, and rescue me: Bow down thine ear unto me, and save me.

3   Be thou to me a rock of habitation, whereunto I may continually resort: Thou hast given commandment to save me; For thou art my rock and my fortress.

4   Rescue me, O my God, out of the hand of the wicked, Out of the hand of the unrighteous and cruel man.

5   For thou art my hope, O Lord Jehovah: Thou art my trust from my youth.

6   By thee have I been holden up from the womb; Thou art he that took me out of my mother's bowels: My praise shall be continually of thee.

7   I am as a wonder unto many; But thou art my strong refuge.

8   My mouth shall be filled with thy praise, And with thy honor all the day.

9   Cast me not off in the time of old age; Forsake me not when my strength faileth.

10   For mine enemies speak concerning me; And they that watch for my soul take counsel together,

11   Saying, God hath forsaken him: Pursue and take him; for there is none to deliver.

12   O God, be not far from me; O my God, make haste to help me.

13 Let them be put to shame and consumed that are adversaries to my soul;
Let them be covered with reproach and dishonor that seek my hurt.

14 But I will hope continually, And will praise thee yet more and more.

15 My mouth shall tell of thy righteousness, And of thy salvation all the day;
For I know not the numbers thereof.

16 I will come with the mighty acts of the Lord Jehovah: I will make mention
of thy righteousness, even of thine only.

17 O God, thou hast taught me from my youth; And hitherto have I declared
thy wondrous works.

18 Yea, even when I am old and grayheaded, O God, forsake me not, Until I
have declared thy strength unto the next generation, Thy might to every
one that is to come.

19 Thy righteousness also, O God, is very high; Thou who hast done great
things, O God, who is like unto thee?

20 Thou, who hast showed us many and sore troubles, Wilt quicken us again,
And wilt bring us up again from the depths of the earth.

21 Increase thou my greatness, And turn again and comfort me.

22 I will also praise thee with the psaltery, Even thy truth, O my God: Unto
thee will I sing praises with the harp, O thou Holy One of Israel.

23 My lips shall shout for joy when I sing praises unto thee; And my soul,
which thou hast redeemed.

24 My tongue also shall talk of thy righteousness all the day long; For they
are put to shame, for they are confounded, that seek my hurt.

Psalm 72

A Psalm of Solomon.

1   Give the king thy judgments, O God, And thy righteousness unto the king's son.

2   He will judge thy people with righteousness, And thy poor with justice.

3   The mountains shall bring peace to the people, And the hills, in righteousness.

4   He will judge the poor of the people, He will save the children of the needy, And will break in pieces the oppressor.

5   They shall fear thee while the sun endureth, And so long as the moon, throughout all generations.

6   He will come down like rain upon the mown grass, As showers that water the earth.

7   In his days shall the righteous flourish, And abundance of peace, till the moon be no more.

8   He shall have dominion also from sea to sea, And from the River unto the ends of the earth.

9   They that dwell in the wilderness shall bow before him; And his enemies shall lick the dust.

10   The kings of Tarshish and of the isles shall render tribute: The kings of Sheba and Seba shall offer gifts.

11   Yea, all kings shall fall down before him; All nations shall serve him.

12 For he will deliver the needy when he crieth, And the poor, that hath no helper.

13 He will have pity on the poor and needy, And the souls of the needy he will save.

14 He will redeem their soul from oppression and violence; And precious will their blood be in his sight:

15 And they shall live; and to him shall be given of the gold of Sheba: And men shall pray for him continually; They shall bless him all the day long.

16 There shall be abundance of grain in the earth upon the top of the mountains; The fruit thereof shall shake like Lebanon: And they of the city shall flourish like grass of the earth.

17 His name shall endure for ever; His name shall be continued as long as the sun: And men shall be blessed in him; All nations shall call him happy.

18 Blessed be Jehovah God, the God of Israel, Who only doeth wondrous things:

19 And blessed be his glorious name for ever; And let the whole earth be filled with his glory. Amen, and Amen.

20 The prayers of David the son of Jesse are ended.

Psalm 73

A Psalm of Asaph.

1 Surely God is good to Israel, Even to such as are pure in heart.

2 But as for me, my feet were almost gone; My steps had well nigh slipped.

3 For I was envious at the arrogant, When I saw the prosperity of the wicked.

4 For there are no pangs in their death; But their strength is firm.

5 They are not in trouble as other men; Neither are they plagued like other men.

6 Therefore pride is as a chain about their neck; Violence covereth them as a garment.

7 Their eyes stand out with fatness: They have more than heart could wish.

8 They scoff, and in wickedness utter oppression: They speak loftily.

9 They have set their mouth in the heavens, And their tongue walketh through the earth.

10 Therefore his people return hither: And waters of a full cup are drained by them.

11 And they say, How doth God know? And is there knowledge in the Most High?

12 Behold, these are the wicked; And, being alway at ease, they increase in riches.

13 Surely in vain have I cleansed my heart, And washed my hands in innocency;

14 For all the day long have I been plagued, And chastened every morning.

15 If I had said, I will speak thus; Behold, I had dealt treacherously with the generation of thy children.

16 When I thought how I might know this, It was too painful for me;

17 Until I went into the sanctuary of God, And considered their latter end.

18 Surely thou settest them in slippery places: Thou castest them down to destruction.

19 How are they become a desolation in a moment! They are utterly consumed with terrors.

20 As a dream when one awaketh, So, O Lord, when thou awakest, thou wilt despise their image.

21 For my soul was grieved, And I was pricked in my heart:

22 So brutish was I, and ignorant; I was as a beast before thee.

23 Nevertheless I am continually with thee: Thou hast holden my right hand.

24 Thou wilt guide me with thy counsel, And afterward receive me to glory.

25 Whom have I in heaven but thee? And there is none upon earth that I desire besides thee.

26 My flesh and my heart faileth; But God is the strength of my heart and my portion for ever.

27 For, lo, they that are far from thee shall perish: Thou hast destroyed all them that play the harlot, departing from thee.

28 But it is good for me to draw near unto God: I have made the Lord Jehovah my refuge, That I may tell of all thy works.

Psalm 74

Maschil of Asaph.

1   O God, why hast thou cast us off for ever? Why doth thine anger smoke against the sheep of thy pasture?

2   Remember thy congregation, which thou hast gotten of old, Which thou hast redeemed to be the tribe of thine inheritance; And mount Zion, wherein thou hast dwelt.

3   Lift up thy feet unto the perpetual ruins, All the evil that the enemy hath done in the sanctuary.

4   Thine adversaries have roared in the midst of thine assembly; They have set up their ensigns for signs.

5   They seemed as men that lifted up Axes upon a thicket of trees.

6   And now all the carved work thereof They break down with hatchet and hammers.

7   They have set thy sanctuary on fire; They have profaned the dwelling-place of thy name by casting it to the ground.

8   They said in their heart, Let us make havoc of them altogether: They have burned up all the synagogues of God in the land.

9   We see not our signs: There is no more any prophet; Neither is there among us any that knoweth how long.

10   How long, O God, shall the adversary reproach? Shall the enemy blaspheme thy name for ever?

11   Why drawest thou back thy hand, even thy right hand? Pluck it out of thy bosom and consume them.

12 Yet God is my King of old, Working salvation in the midst of the earth.

13 Thou didst divide the sea by thy strength: Thou brakest the heads of the sea-monsters in the waters.

14 Thou brakest the heads of leviathan in pieces; Thou gavest him to be food to the people inhabiting the wilderness.

15 Thou didst cleave fountain and flood: Thou driedst up mighty rivers.

16 The day is thine, the night also is thine: Thou hast prepared the light and the sun.

17 Thou hast set all the borders of the earth: Thou hast made summer and winter.

18 Remember this, that the enemy hath reproached, O Jehovah, And that a foolish people hath blasphemed thy name.

19 Oh deliver not the soul of thy turtle-dove unto the wild beast: Forget not the life of thy poor for ever.

20 Have respect unto the covenant; For the dark places of the earth are full of the habitations of violence.

21 Oh let not the oppressed return ashamed: Let the poor and needy praise thy name.

22 Arise, O God, plead thine own cause: Remember how the foolish man reproacheth thee all the day.

23 Forget not the voice of thine adversaries: The tumult of those that rise up against thee ascendeth continually.

Psalm 75

For the Chief Musician; set to Al-tash-heth. A Psalm of Asaph; a song.

1   We give thanks unto thee, O God; We give thanks, for thy name is near: Men tell of thy wondrous works.

2   When I shall find the set time, I will judge uprightly.

3   The earth and all the inhabitants thereof are dissolved: I have set up the pillars of it. Selah

4   I said unto the arrogant, Deal not arrogantly; And to the wicked, Lift not up the horn:

5   Lift not up your horn on high; Speak not with a stiff neck.

6   For neither from the east, nor from the west, Nor yet from the south, cometh lifting up.

7   But God is the judge: He putteth down one, and lifteth up another.

8   For in the hand of Jehovah there is a cup, and the wine foameth; It is full of mixture, and he poureth out of the same: Surely the dregs thereof, all the wicked of the earth shall drain them, and drink them.

9   But I will declare for ever, I will sing praises to the God of Jacob.

10   All the horns of the wicked also will I cut off; But the horns of the righteous shall be lifted up.

Psalm 76

For the Chief Musician; on stringed instruments. A Psalm of Asaph, a song.

1   In Judah is God known: His name is great in Israel.

2   In Salem also is his tabernacle, And his dwelling-place in Zion.

3   There he brake the arrows of the bow; The shield, and the sword, and the battle. Selah

4   Glorious art thou and excellent, From the mountains of prey.

5   The stouthearted are made a spoil, They have slept their sleep; And none of the men of might have found their hands.

6   At thy rebuke, O God of Jacob, Both chariot and horse are cast into a deep sleep.

7   Thou, even thou, art to be feared; And who may stand in thy sight when once thou art angry?

8   Thou didst cause sentence to be heard from heaven; The earth feared, and was still,

9   When God arose to judgment, To save all the meek of the earth. Selah

10   Surely the wrath of man shall praise thee: The residue of wrath shalt thou gird upon thee.

11   Vow, and pay unto Jehovah your God: Let all that are round about him bring presents unto him that ought to be feared.

12   He will cut off the spirit of princes: He is terrible to the kings of the earth.

Psalm 77

For the Chief Musician; after the manner of Jeduthan. A Psalm of Asaph.

1   I will cry unto God with my voice, Even unto God with my voice; and he will give ear unto me.

2   In the day of my trouble I sought the Lord: My hand was stretched out in the night, and slacked not; My soul refused to be comforted.

3   I remember God, and am disquieted: I complain, and my spirit is overwhelmed. Selah

4   Thou holdest mine eyes watching: I am so troubled that I cannot speak.

5   I have considered the days of old, The years of ancient times.

6   I call to remembrance my song in the night: I commune with mine own heart; And my spirit maketh diligent search.

7   Will the Lord cast off for ever? And will he be favorable no more?

8   Is his lovingkindness clean gone for ever? Doth his promise fail for evermore?

9   Hath God forgotten to be gracious? Hath he in anger shut up his tender mercies? Selah

10   And I said, This is my infirmity; But I will remember the years of the right hand of the Most High.

11   I will make mention of the deeds of Jehovah; For I will remember thy wonders of old.

12   I will meditate also upon all thy work, And muse on thy doings.

13   Thy way, O God, is in the sanctuary: Who is a great god like unto God?

14   Thou art the God that doest wonders: Thou hast made known thy strength among the peoples.

15   Thou hast with thine arm redeemed thy people, The sons of Jacob and Joseph. Selah

16   The waters saw thee, O God; The waters saw thee, they were afraid: The depths also trembled.

17   The clouds poured out water; The skies sent out a sound: Thine arrows also went abroad.

18   The voice of thy thunder was in the whirlwind; The lightnings lightened the world: The earth trembled and shook.

19   Thy way was in the sea, And thy paths in the great waters, And thy footsteps were not known.

20   Thou leddest thy people like a flock, By the hand of Moses and Aaron.

Psalm 78

Maschil of Asaph.

1   Give ear, O my people, to my law: Incline your ears to the words of my mouth.

2   I will open my mouth in a parable; I will utter dark sayings of old,

3   Which we have heard and known, And our fathers have told us.

4   We will not hide them from their children, Telling to the generation to come the praises of Jehovah, And his strength, and his wondrous works that he hath done.

5   For he established a testimony in Jacob, And appointed a law in Israel, Which he commanded our fathers, That they should make them known to their children;

6   That the generation to come might know them, even the children that should be born; Who should arise and tell them to their children,

7   That they might set their hope in God, And not forget the works of God, But keep his commandments,

8   And might not be as their fathers, A stubborn and rebellious generation, A generation that set not their heart aright, And whose spirit was not stedfast with God.

9   The children of Ephraim, being armed and carrying bows, Turned back in the day of battle.

10 They kept not the covenant of God, And refused to walk in his law;

11 And they forgat his doings, And his wondrous works that he had showed them.

12 Marvellous things did he in the sight of their fathers, In the land of Egypt, in the field of Zoan.

13 He clave the sea, and caused them to pass through; And he made the waters to stand as a heap.

14 In the day-time also he led them with a cloud, And all the night with a light of fire.

15 He clave rocks in the wilderness, And gave them drink abundantly as out of the depths.

16 He brought streams also out of the rock, And caused waters to run down like rivers.

17 Yet went they on still to sin against him, To rebel against the Most High in the desert.

18 And they tempted God in their heart By asking food according to their desire.

19 Yea, they spake against God; They said, Can God prepare a table in the wilderness?

20 Behold, he smote the rock, so that waters gushed out, And streams overflowed; Can he give bread also? Will he provide flesh for his people?

21 Therefore Jehovah heard, and was wroth; And a fire was kindled against Jacob, And anger also went up against Israel;

22 Because they believed not in God, And trusted not in his salvation.

23 Yet he commanded the skies above, And opened the doors of heaven;

24 And he rained down manna upon them to eat, And gave them food from heaven.

25 Man did eat the bread of the mighty: He sent them food to the full.

²⁶ He caused the east wind to blow in the heavens; And by his power he guided the south wind.

²⁷ He rained flesh also upon them as the dust, And winged birds as the sand of the seas:

²⁸ And he let it fall in the midst of their camp, Round about their habitations.

²⁹ So they did eat, and were well filled; And he gave them their own desire.

³⁰ They were not estranged from that which they desired, Their food was yet in their mouths,

³¹ When the anger of God went up against them, And slew of the fattest of them, And smote down the young men of Israel.

³² For all this they sinned still, And believed not in his wondrous works.

³³ Therefore their days did he consume in vanity, And their years in terror.

³⁴ When he slew them, then they inquired after him; And they returned and sought God earnestly.

³⁵ And they remembered that God was their rock, And the Most High God their redeemer.

³⁶ But they flattered him with their mouth, And lied unto him with their tongue.

³⁷ For their heart was not right with him, Neither were they faithful in his covenant.

³⁸ But he, being merciful, forgave their iniquity, and destroyed them not: Yea, many a time turned he his anger away, And did not stir up all his wrath.

³⁹ And he remembered that they were but flesh, A wind that passeth away, and cometh not again.

40 How oft did they rebel against him in the wilderness, And grieve him in the desert!

41 And they turned again and tempted God, And provoked the Holy One of Israel.

42 They remember not his hand, Nor the day when he redeemed them from the adversary;

43 How he set his signs in Egypt, And his wonders in the field of Zoan,

44 And turned their rivers into blood, And their streams, so that they could not drink.

45 He sent among them swarms of flies, which devoured them; And frogs, which destroyed them.

46 He gave also their increase unto the caterpillar, And their labor unto the locust.

47 He destroyed their vines with hail, And their sycomore-trees with frost.

48 He gave over their cattle also to the hail, And their flocks to hot thunderbolts.

49 He cast upon them the fierceness of his anger, Wrath, and indignation, and trouble, A band of angels of evil.

50 He made a path for his anger; He spared not their soul from death, But gave their life over to the pestilence,

51 And smote all the first-born in Egypt, The chief of their strength in the tents of Ham.

52 But he led forth his own people like sheep, And guided them in the wilderness like a flock.

53 And he led them safely, so that they feared not; But the sea overwhelmed their enemies.

54   And he brought them to the border of his sanctuary, To this mountain, which his right hand had gotten.

55   He drove out the nations also before them, And allotted them for an inheritance by line, And made the tribes of Israel to dwell in their tents.

56   Yet they tempted and rebelled against the Most High God, And kept not his testimonies;

57   But turned back, and dealt treacherously like their fathers: They were turned aside like a deceitful bow.

58   For they provoked him to anger with their high places, And moved him to jealousy with their graven images.

59   When God heard this, he was wroth, And greatly abhorred Israel;

60   So that he forsook the tabernacle of Shiloh, The tent which he placed among men;

61   And delivered his strength into captivity, And his glory into the adversary's hand.

62   He gave his people over also unto the sword, And was wroth with his inheritance.

63   Fire devoured their young men; And their virgins had no marriage-song.

64   Their priests fell by the sword; And their widows made no lamentation.

65   Then the Lord awaked as one out of sleep, Like a mighty man that shouteth by reason of wine.

66   And he smote his adversaries backward: He put them to a perpetual reproach.

67 Moreover he refused the tent of Joseph, And chose not the tribe of Ephraim,

68 But chose the tribe of Judah, The mount Zion which he loved.

69 And he built his sanctuary like the heights, Like the earth which he hath established for ever.

70 He chose David also his servant, And took him from the sheepfolds:

71 From following the ewes that have their young he brought him, To be the shepherd of Jacob his people, and Israel his inheritance.

72 So he was their shepherd according to the integrity of his heart, And guided them by the skilfulness of his hands.

Psalm 79

A Psalm of Asaph.

1   O God, the nations are come into thine inheritance; Thy holy temple have they defiled; They have laid Jerusalem in heaps.

2   The dead bodies of thy servants have they given to be food unto the birds of the heavens, The flesh of thy saints unto the beasts of the earth.

3   Their blood have they shed like water round about Jerusalem; And there was none to bury them.

4   We are become a reproach to our neighbors, A scoffing and derision to them that are round about us.

5   How long, O Jehovah? wilt thou be angry for ever? Shall thy jealousy burn like fire?

6   Pour out thy wrath upon the nations that know thee not, And upon the kingdoms that call not upon thy name.

7   For they have devoured Jacob, And laid waste his habitation.

8   Remember not against us the iniquities of our forefathers: Let thy tender mercies speedily meet us; For we are brought very low.

9   Help us, O God of our salvation, for the glory of thy name; And deliver us, and forgive our sins, for thy name's sake.

10   Wherefore should the nations say, Where is their God? Let the avenging of the blood of thy servants which is shed Be known among the nations in our sight.

11   Let the sighing of the prisoner come before thee: According to the greatness of thy power preserve thou those that are appointed to death;

12 And render unto our neighbors sevenfold into their bosom Their reproach, wherewith they have reproached thee, O Lord.

13 So we thy people and sheep of thy pasture Will give thee thanks for ever: We will show forth thy praise to all generations.

Psalm 80

For the Chief Musician, set to Shoshanim Eduth. A Psalm of Asaph.

1 Give ear, O Shepherd of Israel, Thou that leadest Joseph like a flock; Thou that sittest above the cherubim, shine forth.

2 Before Ephraim and Benjamin and Manasseh, stir up thy might, And come to save us.

3 Turn us again, O God; And cause thy face to shine, and we shall be saved.

4 O Jehovah God of hosts, How long wilt thou be angry against the prayer of thy people?

5 Thou hast fed them with the bread of tears, And given them tears to drink in large measure.

6 Thou makest us a strife unto our neighbors; And our enemies laugh among themselves.

7 Turn us again, O God of hosts; And cause thy face to shine, and we shall be saved.

8 Thou broughtest a vine out of Egypt: Thou didst drive out the nations, and plantedst it.

9 Thou preparedst room before it, And it took deep root, and filled the land.

10 The mountains were covered with the shadow of it, And the boughs thereof were like cedars of God.

11 It sent out its branches unto the sea, And its shoots unto the River.

12   Why hast thou broken down its walls, So that all they that pass by the way do pluck it?

13   The boar out of the wood doth ravage it, And the wild beasts of the field feed on it.

14   Turn again, we beseech thee, O God of hosts: Look down from heaven, and behold, and visit this vine,

15   And the stock which thy right hand planted, And the branch that thou madest strong for thyself.

16   It is burned with fire, it is cut down: They perish at the rebuke of thy countenance.

17   Let thy hand be upon the man of thy right hand, Upon the son of man whom thou madest strong for thyself.

18   So shall we not go back from thee: Quicken thou us, and we will call upon thy name.

19   Turn us again, O Jehovah God of hosts; Cause thy face to shine, and we shall be saved.

Psalm 81

For the Chief Musician; set to the Gittith. A Psalm of Asaph.

1   Sing aloud unto God our strength: Make a joyful noise unto the God of Jacob.

2   Raise a song, and bring hither the timbrel, The pleasant harp with the psaltery.

3   Blow the trumpet at the new moon, At the full moon, on our feast-day.

4   For it is a statute for Israel, An ordinance of the God of Jacob.

5   He appointed it in Joseph for a testimony, When he went out over the land of Egypt, Where I heard a language that I knew not.

6   I removed his shoulder from the burden: His hands were freed from the basket.

7   Thou calledst in trouble, and I delivered thee; I answered thee in the secret place of thunder; I proved thee at the waters of Meribah. Selah

8   Hear, O my people, and I will testify unto thee: O Israel, if thou wouldest hearken unto me!

9   There shall no strange god be in thee; Neither shalt thou worship any foreign god.

10 I am Jehovah thy God, Who brought thee up out of the land of Egypt: Open thy mouth wide, and I will fill it.

11 But my people hearkened not to my voice; And Israel would none of me.

12   So I let them go after the stubbornness of their heart, That they might walk in their own counsels.

13   Oh that my people would hearken unto me, That Israel would walk in my ways!

14   I would soon subdue their enemies, And turn my hand against their adversaries.

15   The haters of Jehovah should submit themselves unto him: But their time should endure for ever.

16   He would feed them also with the finest of the wheat; And with honey out of the rock would I satisfy thee.

Psalm 82

A Psalm of Asaph.

1   God standeth in the congregation of God; He judgeth among the gods.

2   How long will ye judge unjustly, And respect the persons of the wicked? Selah

3   Judge the poor and fatherless: Do justice to the afflicted and destitute.

4   Rescue the poor and needy: Deliver them out of the hand of the wicked.

5   They know not, neither do they understand; They walk to and fro in darkness: All the foundations of the earth are shaken.

6   I said, Ye are gods, And all of you sons of the Most High.

7   Nevertheless ye shall die like men, And fall like one of the princes.

8   Arise, O God, judge the earth; For thou shalt inherit all the nations.

Psalm 83

A song. A Psalm of Asaph.

1 O God, keep not thou silence: Hold not thy peace, and be not still, O God.

2 For, lo, thine enemies make a tumult; And they that hate thee have lifted up the head.

3 Thy take crafty counsel against thy people, And consult together against thy hidden ones.

4 They have said, Come, and let us cut them off from being a nation; That the name of Israel may be no more in remembrance.

5 For they have consulted together with one consent; Against thee do they make a covenant:

6 The tents of Edom and the Ishmaelites; Moab, and the Hagarenes;

7 Gebal, and Ammon, and Amalek; Philistia with the inhabitants of Tyre:

8 Assyria also is joined with them; They have helped the children of Lot. Selah

9 Do thou unto them as unto Midian, As to Sisera, as to Jabin, at the river Kishon;

10 Who perished at Endor, Who became as dung for the earth.

11 Make their nobles like Oreb and Zeeb; Yea, all their princes like Zebah and Zalmunna;

12 Who said, Let us take to ourselves in possession The habitations of God.

13 O my God, make them like the whirling dust; As stubble before the wind.

14 As the fire that burneth the forest, And as the flame that setteth the mountains on fire,

15 So pursue them with thy tempest, And terrify them with thy storm.

16 Fill their faces with confusion, That they may seek thy name, O Jehovah.

17 Let them be put to shame and dismayed for ever; Yea, let them be confounded and perish;

18 That they may know that thou alone, whose name is Jehovah, Art the Most High over all the earth.

Psalm 84

For the Chief Musician; set to the Gittith. A Psalm of the sons of Korah.

1 How amiable are thy tabernacles, O Jehovah of hosts!

2 My soul longeth, yea, even fainteth for the courts of Jehovah; My heart and my flesh cry out unto the living God.

3 Yea, the sparrow hath found her a house, And the swallow a nest for herself, where she may lay her young, Even thine altars, O Jehovah of hosts, My King, and my God.

4 Blessed are they that dwell in thy house: They will be still praising thee. Selah

5 Blessed is the man whose strength is in thee; In whose heart are the highways to Zion.

6 Passing through the valley of Weeping they make it a place of springs; Yea, the early rain covereth it with blessings.

7 They go from strength to strength; Every one of them appeareth before God in Zion.

8 O Jehovah God of hosts, hear my prayer; Give ear, O God of Jacob. Selah

9 Behold, O God our shield, And look upon the face of thine anointed.

10 For a day in thy courts is better than a thousand. I had rather be a doorkeeper in the house of my God, Than to dwell in the tents of wickedness.

11 For Jehovah God is a sun and a shield: Jehovah will give grace and glory; No good thing will he withhold from them that walk uprightly.

12 O Jehovah of hosts, Blessed is the man that trusteth in thee.

Psalm 85

For the Chief Musician. A Psalm of the sons of Korah.

1   Jehovah, thou hast been favorable unto thy land; Thou hast brought back the captivity of Jacob.

2   Thou hast forgiven the iniquity of thy people; Thou hast covered all their sin. Selah

3   Thou hast taken away all thy wrath; Thou hast turned thyself from the fierceness of thine anger.

4   Turn us, O God of our salvation, And cause thine indignation toward us to cease.

5   Wilt thou be angry with us for ever? Wilt thou draw out thine anger to all generations?

6   Wilt thou not quicken us again, That thy people may rejoice in thee?

7   Show us thy lovingkindness, O Jehovah, And grant us thy salvation.

8   I will hear what God Jehovah will speak; For he will speak peace unto his people, and to his saints: But let them not turn again to folly.

9   Surely his salvation is nigh them that fear him, That glory may dwell in our land.

10   Mercy and truth are met together; Righteousness and peace have kissed each other.

11   Truth springeth out of the earth; And righteousness hath looked down from heaven.

12   Yea, Jehovah will give that which is good; And our land shall yield its increase.

13   Righteousness shall go before him, And shall make his footsteps a way to walk in.

Psalm 86

A Prayer of David

1   Bow down thine ear, O Jehovah, and answer me; For I am poor and needy.

2   Preserve my soul; for I am godly: O thou my God, save thy servant that trusteth in thee.

3   Be merciful unto me, O Lord; For unto thee do I cry all the day long.

4   Rejoice the soul of thy servant; For unto thee, O Lord, do I lift up my soul.

5   For thou, Lord, art good, and ready to forgive, And abundant in lovingkindness unto all them that call upon thee.

6   Give ear, O Jehovah, unto my prayer; And hearken unto the voice of my supplications.

7   In the day of my trouble I will call upon thee; For thou wilt answer me.

8   There is none like unto thee among the gods, O Lord; Neither are there any works like unto thy works.

9   All nations whom thou hast made shall come and worship before thee, O Lord; And they shall glorify thy name.

10   For thou art great, and doest wondrous things: Thou art God alone.

11   Teach me thy way, O Jehovah; I will walk in thy truth: Unite my heart to fear thy name.

12 I will praise thee, O Lord my God, with my whole heart; And I will glorify thy name for evermore.

13 For great is thy lovingkindness toward me; And thou hast delivered my soul from the lowest Sheol.

14 O God, the proud are risen up against me, And a company of violent men have sought after my soul, And have not set thee before them.

15 But thou, O Lord, art a God merciful and gracious, Slow to anger, and abundant in lovingkindness and truth.

16 Oh turn unto me, and have mercy upon me; Give thy strength unto thy servant, And save the son of thy handmaid.

17 Show me a token for good, That they who hate me may see it, and be put to shame, Because thou, Jehovah, hast helped me, and comforted me.

Psalm 87

A Psalm of the sons of Korah; a Song.

1   His foundation is in the holy mountains.

2   Jehovah loveth the gates of Zion More than all the dwellings of Jacob.

3   Glorious things are spoken of thee, O city of God. Selah

4   I will make mention of Rahab and Babylon as among them that know me: Behold, Philistia, and Tyre, with Ethiopia: This one was born there.

5   Yea, of Zion it shall be said, This one and that one was born in her; And the Most High himself will establish her.

6   Jehovah will count, when he writeth up the peoples, This one was born there. Selah

7   They that sing as well as they that dance shall say, All my fountains are in thee.

Psalm 88

A Song, a Psalm of the sons of Korah; for the Chief Musician; set to Mahalath Leannoth. Maschil of Heman the Ezrahite.

1 O Jehovah, the God of my salvation, I have cried day and night before thee.

2 Let my prayer enter into thy presence; Incline thine ear unto my cry.

3 For my soul is full of troubles, And my life draweth nigh unto Sheol.

4 I am reckoned with them that go down into the pit; I am as a man that hath no help,

5 Cast off among the dead, Like the slain that lie in the grave, Whom thou rememberest no more, And they are cut off from thy hand.

6 Thou hast laid me in the lowest pit, In dark places, in the deeps.

7 Thy wrath lieth hard upon me, And thou hast afflicted me with all thy waves. Selah

8 Thou hast put mine acquaintance far from me; Thou hast made me an abomination unto them: I am shut up, and I cannot come forth.

9 Mine eye wasteth away by reason of affliction: I have called daily upon thee, O Jehovah; I have spread forth my hands unto thee.

10 Wilt thou show wonders to the dead? Shall they that are decreased arise and praise thee? Selah

11 Shall thy lovingkindness be declared in the grave? Or thy faithfulness in Destruction?

¹² Shall thy wonders be known in the dark? And thy righteousness in the land of forgetfulness?

¹³ But unto thee, O Jehovah, have I cried; And in the morning shall my prayer come before thee.

¹⁴ Jehovah, why castest thou off my soul? Why hidest thou thy face from me?

¹⁵ I am afflicted and ready to die from my youth up: While I suffer thy terrors I am distracted.

¹⁶ Thy fierce wrath is gone over me; Thy terrors have cut me off.

¹⁷ They came round about me like water all the day long; They compassed me about together.

¹⁸ Lover and friend hast thou put far from me, And mine acquaintance into darkness.

Psalm 89

Maschil of Ethan the Ezrahite.

1 I will sing of the lovingkindness of Jehovah for ever: With my mouth will I make known thy faithfulness to all generations.

2 For I have said, Mercy shall be built up for ever; Thy faithfulness wilt thou establish in the very heavens.

3 I have made a covenant with my chosen, I have sworn unto David my servant:

4 Thy seed will I establish for ever, And build up thy throne to all generations. Selah

5 And the heavens shall praise thy wonders, O Jehovah; Thy faithfulness also in the assembly of the holy ones.

6 For who in the skies can be compared unto Jehovah? Who among the sons of the mighty is like unto Jehovah,

7 A God very terrible in the council of the holy ones, And to be feared above all them that are round about him?

8 O Jehovah God of hosts, Who is a mighty one, like unto thee, O Jehovah? And thy faithfulness is round about thee.

9 Thou rulest the pride of the sea: When the waves thereof arise, thou stillest them.

10 Thou hast broken Rahab in pieces, as one that is slain; Thou hast scattered thine enemies with the arm of thy strength.

11 The heavens are thine, the earth also is thine: The world and the fulness thereof, thou hast founded them.

¹² The north and the south, thou hast created them: Tabor and Hermon rejoice in thy name.

¹³ Thou hast a mighty arm; Strong is thy hand, and high is thy right hand.

¹⁴ Righteousness and justice are the foundation of thy throne: Lovingkindness and truth go before thy face.

¹⁵ Blessed is the people that know the joyful sound: They walk, O Jehovah, in the light of thy countenance.

¹⁶ In thy name do they rejoice all the day; And in thy righteousness are they exalted.

¹⁷ For thou art the glory of their strength; And in thy favor our horn shall be exalted.

¹⁸ For our shield belongeth unto Jehovah; And our king to the Holy One of Israel.

¹⁹ Then thou spakest in vision to thy saints, And saidst, I have laid help upon one that is mighty; I have exalted one chosen out of the people.

²⁰ I have found David my servant; With my holy oil have I anointed him:

²¹ With whom my hand shall be established; Mine arm also shall strengthen him.

²² The enemy shall not exact from him, Nor the son of wickedness afflict him.

²³ And I will beat down his adversaries before him, And smite them that hate him.

²⁴ But my faithfulness and my lovingkindness shall be with him; And in my name shall his horn be exalted.

²⁵ I will set his hand also on the sea, And his right hand on the rivers.

26 He shall cry unto me, Thou art my Father, My God, and the rock of my salvation.

27 I also will make him my first-born, The highest of the kings of the earth.

28 My lovingkindness will I keep for him for evermore; And my covenant shall stand fast with him.

29 His seed also will I make to endure for ever, And his throne as the days of heaven.

30 If his children forsake my law, And walk not in mine ordinances;

31 If they break my statutes, And keep not my commandments;

32 Then will I visit their transgression with the rod, And their iniquity with stripes.

33 But my lovingkindness will I not utterly take from him, Nor suffer my faithfulness to fail.

34 My covenant will I not break, Nor alter the thing that is gone out of my lips.

35 Once have I sworn by my holiness: I will not lie unto David:

36 His seed shall endure for ever, And his throne as the sun before me.

37 It shall be established for ever as the moon, And as the faithful witness in the sky. Selah

38 But thou hast cast off and rejected, Thou hast been wroth with thine anointed.

39 Thou hast abhorred the covenant of thy servant: Thou hast profaned his crown by casting it to the ground.

40 Thou hast broken down all his hedges; Thou hast brought his strongholds to ruin.

41   All that pass by the way rob him: He is become a reproach to his neighbors.

42   Thou hast exalted the right hand of his adversaries; Thou hast made all his enemies to rejoice.

43   Yea, thou turnest back the edge of his sword, And hast not made him to stand in the battle.

44   Thou hast made his brightness to cease, And cast his throne down to the ground.

45   The days of his youth hast thou shortened: Thou hast covered him with shame. Selah

46   How long, O Jehovah? wilt thou hide thyself for ever? How long shall thy wrath burn like fire?

47   Oh remember how short my time is: For what vanity hast thou created all the children of men!

48   What man is he that shall live and not see death, That shall deliver his soul from the power of Sheol? Selah

49   Lord, where are thy former lovingkindnesses, Which thou swarest unto David in thy faithfulness?

50   Remember, Lord, the reproach of thy servants; How I do bear in my bosom the reproach of all the mighty peoples,

51   Wherewith thine enemies have reproached, O Jehovah, Wherewith they have reproached the footsteps of thine anointed.

52   Blessed be Jehovah for evermore. Amen, and Amen.

Psalm 90

A Prayer of Moses the man of God.

1 Lord, thou hast been our dwelling-place In all generations.

2 Before the mountains were brought forth, Or ever thou hadst formed the earth and the world, Even from everlasting to everlasting, thou art God.

3 Thou turnest man to destruction, And sayest, Return, ye children of men.

4 For a thousand years in thy sight Are but as yesterday when it is past, And as a watch in the night.

5 Thou carriest them away as with a flood; they are as a sleep: In the morning they are like grass which groweth up.

6 In the morning it flourisheth, and groweth up; In the evening it is cut down, and withereth.

7 For we are consumed in thine anger, And in thy wrath are we troubled.

8 Thou hast set our iniquities before thee, Our secret sins in the light of thy countenance.

9 For all our days are passed away in thy wrath: We bring our years to an end as a sigh.

10 The days of our years are threescore years and ten, Or even by reason of strength fourscore years; Yet is their pride but labor and sorrow; For it is soon gone, and we fly away.

11 Who knoweth the power of thine anger, And thy wrath according to the fear that is due unto thee?

12   So teach us to number our days, That we may get us a heart of wisdom.

13   Return, O Jehovah; how long? And let it repent thee concerning thy servants.

14   Oh satisfy us in the morning with thy lovingkindness, That we may rejoice and be glad all our days.

15   Make us glad according to the days wherein thou hast afflicted us, And the years wherein we have seen evil.

16   Let thy work appear unto thy servants, And thy glory upon their children.

17   And let the favor of the Lord our God be upon us; And establish thou the work of our hands upon us; Yea, the work of our hands establish thou it.

Psalm 91

1 He that dwelleth in the secret place of the Most High Shall abide under the shadow of the Almighty.

2 I will say of Jehovah, He is my refuge and my fortress; My God, in whom I trust.

3 For he will deliver thee from the snare of the fowler, And from the deadly pestilence.

4 He will cover thee with his pinions, And under his wings shalt thou take refuge: His truth is a shield and a buckler.

5 Thou shalt not be afraid for the terror by night, Nor for the arrow that flieth by day;

6 For the pestilence that walketh in darkness, Nor for the destruction that wasteth at noonday.

7 A thousand shall fall at thy side, And ten thousand at thy right hand; But it shall not come nigh thee.

8 Only with thine eyes shalt thou behold, And see the reward of the wicked.

9 For thou, O Jehovah, art my refuge! Thou hast made the Most High thy habitation;

10 There shall no evil befall thee, Neither shall any plague come nigh thy tent.

11 For he will give his angels charge over thee, To keep thee in all thy ways.

¹² They shall bear thee up in their hands, Lest thou dash thy foot against a stone.

¹³ Thou shalt tread upon the lion and adder: The young lion and the serpent shalt thou trample under foot.

¹⁴ Because he hath set his love upon me, therefore will I deliver him: I will set him on high, because he hath known my name.

¹⁵ He shall call upon me, and I will answer him; I will be with him in trouble: I will deliver him, and honor him.

¹⁶ With long life will I satisfy him, And show him my salvation.

Psalm 92

A Psalm, a Song for the sabbath day.

1 It is a good thing to give thanks unto Jehovah, And to sing praises unto thy name, O Most High;

2 To show forth thy lovingkindness in the morning, And thy faithfulness every night,

3 With an instrument of ten strings, and with the psaltery; With a solemn sound upon the harp.

4 For thou, Jehovah, hast made me glad through thy work: I will triumph in the works of thy hands.

5 How great are thy works, O Jehovah! Thy thoughts are very deep.

6 A brutish man knoweth not; Neither doth a fool understand this:

7 When the wicked spring as the grass, And when all the workers of iniquity do flourish; It is that they shall be destroyed for ever.

8 But thou, O Jehovah, art on high for evermore.

9 For, lo, thine enemies, O Jehovah, For, lo, thine enemies shall perish; All the workers of iniquity shall be scattered.

10 But my horn hast thou exalted like the horn of the wild-ox: I am anointed with fresh oil.

11 Mine eye also hath seen my desire on mine enemies, Mine ears have heard my desire of the evil-doers that rise up against me.

12 The righteous shall flourish like the palm-tree: He shall grow like a cedar in Lebanon.

13   They are planted in the house of Jehovah; They shall flourish in the courts of our God.

14   They shall still bring forth fruit in old age; They shall be full of sap and green:

15   To show that Jehovah is upright; He is my rock, and there is no unrighteousness in him.

Psalm 93

1   Jehovah reigneth; he is clothed with majesty; Jehovah is clothed with strength; he hath girded himself therewith: The world also is established, that it cannot be moved.

2   Thy throne is established of old: Thou art from everlasting.

3   The floods have lifted up, O Jehovah, The floods have lifted up their voice; The floods lift up their waves.

4   Above the voices of many waters, The mighty breakers of the sea, Jehovah on high is mighty.

5   Thy testimonies are very sure: Holiness becometh thy house, O Jehovah, for evermore.

Psalm 94

1   O Jehovah, thou God to whom vengeance belongeth, Thou God to whom vengeance belongeth, shine forth.

2   Lift up thyself, thou judge of the earth: Render to the proud their desert.

3   Jehovah, how long shall the wicked, How long shall the wicked triumph?

4   They prate, they speak arrogantly: All the workers of iniquity boast themselves.

5   They break in pieces thy people, O Jehovah, And afflict thy heritage.

6   They slay the widow and the sojourner, And murder the fatherless.

7   And they say, Jehovah will not see, Neither will the God of Jacob consider.

8   Consider, ye brutish among the people; And ye fools, when will ye be wise?

9   He that planted the ear, shall he not hear? He that formed the eye, shall he not see?

10   He that chastiseth the nations, shall not he correct, Even he that teacheth man knowledge?

11   Jehovah knoweth the thoughts of man, That they are vanity.

12   Blessed is the man whom thou chastenest, O Jehovah, And teachest out of thy law;

13 That thou mayest give him rest from the days of adversity, Until the pit be digged for the wicked.

14 For Jehovah will not cast off his people, Neither will he forsake his inheritance.

15 For judgment shall return unto righteousness; And all the upright in heart shall follow it.

16 Who will rise up for me against the evil-doers? Who will stand up for me against the workers of iniquity?

17 Unless Jehovah had been my help, My soul had soon dwelt in silence.

18 When I said, My foot slippeth; Thy lovingkindness, O Jehovah, held me up.

19 In the multitude of my thoughts within me Thy comforts delight my soul.

20 Shall the throne of wickedness have fellowship with thee, Which frameth mischief by statute?

21 They gather themselves together against the soul of the righteous, And condemn the innocent blood.

22 But Jehovah hath been my high tower, And my God the rock of my refuge.

23 And he hath brought upon them their own iniquity, And will cut them off in their own wickedness; Jehovah our God will cut them off.

Psalm 95

1 Oh come, let us sing unto Jehovah; Let us make a joyful noise to the rock of our salvation.

2 Let us come before his presence with thanksgiving; Let us make a joyful noise unto him with Psalms.

3 For Jehovah is a great God, And a great King above all gods.

4 In his hand are the deep places of the earth; The heights of the mountains are his also.

5 The sea is his, and he made it; And his hands formed the dry land.

6 Oh come, let us worship and bow down; Let us kneel before Jehovah our Maker:

7 For he is our God, And we are the people of his pasture, and the sheep of his hand. To-day, oh that ye would hear his voice!

8 Harden not your heart, as at Meribah, As in the day of Massah in the wilderness;

9 When your fathers tempted me, Proved me, and saw my work.

10 Forty years long was I grieved with that generation, And said, It is a people that do err in their heart, And they have not known my ways:

11 Wherefore I sware in my wrath, That they should not enter into my rest.

Psalm 96

1   Oh sing unto Jehovah a new song: Sing unto Jehovah, all the earth.

2   Sing unto Jehovah, bless his name; Show forth his salvation from day to day.

3   Declare his glory among the nations, His marvellous works among all the peoples.

4   For great is Jehovah, and greatly to be praised: He is to be feared above all gods.

5   For all the gods of the peoples are idols; But Jehovah made the heavens.

6   Honor and majesty are before him: Strength and beauty are in his sanctuary.

7   Ascribe unto Jehovah, ye kindreds of the peoples, Ascribe unto Jehovah glory and strength.

8   Ascribe unto Jehovah the glory due unto his name: Bring an offering, and come into his courts.

9   Oh worship Jehovah in holy array: Tremble before him, all the earth.

10 Say among the nations, Jehovah reigneth: The world also is established that it cannot be moved: He will judge the peoples with equity.

11 Let the heavens be glad, and let the earth rejoice; Let the sea roar, and the fulness thereof;

12 Let the field exult, and all that is therein; Then shall all the trees of the wood sing for joy

13 Before Jehovah; for he cometh, For he cometh to judge the earth: He will judge the world with righteousness, And the peoples with his truth.

Psalm 97

1   Jehovah reigneth; let the earth rejoice; Let the multitude of isles be glad.

2   Clouds and darkness are round about him: Righteousness and justice are the foundation of his throne.

3   A fire goeth before him, And burneth up his adversaries round about.

4   His lightnings lightened the world: The earth saw, and trembled.

5   The mountains melted like wax at the presence of Jehovah, At the presence of the Lord of the whole earth.

6   The heavens declare his righteousness, And all the peoples have seen his glory.

7   Let all them be put to shame that serve graven images, That boast themselves of idols: Worship him, all ye gods.

8   Zion heard and was glad, And the daughters of Judah rejoiced, Because of thy judgments, O Jehovah.

9   For thou, Jehovah, art most high above all the earth: Thou art exalted far above all gods.

10   O ye that love Jehovah, hate evil: He preserveth the souls of his saints; He delivereth them out of the hand of the wicked.

11   Light is sown for the righteous, And gladness for the upright in heart.

12   Be glad in Jehovah, ye righteous; And give thanks to his holy memorial name.

Psalm 98

A Psalm.

1   Oh sing unto Jehovah a new song; For he hath done marvellous things: His right hand, and his holy arm, hath wrought salvation for him.

2   Jehovah hath made known his salvation: His righteousness hath he openly showed in the sight of the nations.

3   He hath remembered his lovingkindness and his faithfulness toward the house of Israel: All the ends of the earth have seen the salvation of our God.

4   Make a joyful noise unto Jehovah, all the earth: Break forth and sing for joy, yea, sing praises.

5   Sing praises unto Jehovah with the harp; With the harp and the voice of melody.

6   With trumpets and sound of cornet Make a joyful noise before the King, Jehovah.

7   Let the sea roar, and the fulness thereof; The world, and they that dwell therein;

8   Let the floods clap their hands; Let the hills sing for joy together

9   Before Jehovah; for he cometh to judge the earth: He will judge the world with righteousness, And the peoples with equity.

Psalm 99

1   Jehovah reigneth; let the peoples tremble: He sitteth above the cherubim; let the earth be moved.

2   Jehovah is great in Zion; And he is high above all the peoples.

3   Let them praise thy great and terrible name: Holy is he.

4   The king's strength also loveth justice; Thou dost establish equity; Thou executest justice and righteousness in Jacob.

5   Exalt ye Jehovah our God, And worship at his footstool: Holy is he.

6   Moses and Aaron among his priests, And Samuel among them that call upon his name; They called upon Jehovah, and he answered them.

7   He spake unto them in the pillar of cloud: They kept his testimonies, And the statute that he gave them.

8   Thou answeredst them, O Jehovah our God: Thou wast a God that forgavest them, Though thou tookest vengeance of their doings.

9   Exalt ye Jehovah our God, And worship at his holy hill; For Jehovah our God is holy.

Psalm 100

A Psalm of thanksgiving.

1 Make a joyful noise unto Jehovah, all ye lands.

2 Serve Jehovah with gladness: Come before his presence with singing.

3 Know ye that Jehovah, he is God: It is he that hath made us, and we are his; We are his people, and the sheep of his pasture.

4 Enter into his gates with thanksgiving, And into his courts with praise: Give thanks unto him, and bless his name.

5 For Jehovah is good; his lovingkindness endureth for ever, And his faithfulness unto all generations.

Psalm 101

A Psalm of David.

1 I will sing of lovingkindness and justice: Unto thee, O Jehovah, will I sing praises.

2 I will behave myself wisely in a perfect way: Oh when wilt thou come unto me? I will walk within my house with a perfect heart.

3 I will set no base thing before mine eyes: I hate the work of them that turn aside; It shall not cleave unto me.

4 A perverse heart shall depart from me: I will know no evil thing.

5 Whoso privily slandereth his neighbor, him will I destroy: Him that hath a high look and a proud heart will I not suffer.

6 Mine eyes shall be upon the faithful of the land, that they may dwell with me: He that walketh in a perfect way, he shall minister unto me.

7 He that worketh deceit shall not dwell within my house: He that speaketh falsehood shall not be established before mine eyes.

8 Morning by morning will I destroy all the wicked of the land; To cut off all the workers of iniquity from the city of Jehovah.

Psalm 102

A Prayer of the afflicted, when he is overwhelmed, and poureth out his complaint before Jehovah.

1   Hear my prayer, O Jehovah, And let my cry come unto thee.

2   Hide not thy face from me in the day of my distress: Incline thine ear unto me; In the day when I call answer me speedily.

3   For my days consume away like smoke, And my bones are burned as a firebrand.

4   My heart is smitten like grass, and withered; For I forget to eat my bread.

5   By reason of the voice of my groaning My bones cleave to my flesh.

6   I am like a pelican of the wilderness; I am become as an owl of the waste places.

7   I watch, and am become like a sparrow That is alone upon the house-top.

8   Mine enemies reproach me all the day; They that are mad against me do curse by me.

9   For I have eaten ashes like bread, And mingled my drink with weeping,

10 Because of thine indignation and thy wrath: For thou hast taken me up, and cast me away.

11 My days are like a shadow that declineth; And I am withered like grass.

12 But thou, O Jehovah, wilt abide for ever; And thy memorial name unto all generations.

13   Thou wilt arise, and have mercy upon Zion; For it is time to have pity upon her, Yea, the set time is come.

14   For thy servants take pleasure in her stones, And have pity upon her dust.

15   So the nations shall fear the name of Jehovah, And all the kings of the earth thy glory.

16   For Jehovah hath built up Zion; He hath appeared in his glory.

17   He hath regarded the prayer of the destitute, And hath not despised their prayer.

18   This shall be written for the generation to come; And a people which shall be created shall praise Jehovah.

19   For he hath looked down from the height of his sanctuary; From heaven did Jehovah behold the earth;

20   To hear the sighing of the prisoner; To loose those that are appointed to death;

21   That men may declare the name of Jehovah in Zion, And his praise in Jerusalem;

22   When the peoples are gathered together, And the kingdoms, to serve Jehovah.

23   He weakened my strength in the way; He shortened my days.

24   I said, O my God, take me not away in the midst of my days: Thy years are throughout all generations.

25   Of old didst thou lay the foundation of the earth; And the heavens are the work of thy hands.

26 They shall perish, but thou shalt endure; Yea, all of them shall wax old like a garment; As a vesture shalt thou change them, and they shall be changed:

27 But thou art the same, And thy years shall have no end.

28 The children of thy servants shall continue, And their seed shall be established before thee.

Psalm 103

A Psalm of David.

1 Bless Jehovah, O my soul; And all that is within me, bless his holy name.

2 Bless Jehovah, O my soul, And forget not all his benefits:

3 Who forgiveth all thine iniquities; Who healeth all thy diseases;

4 Who redeemeth thy life from destruction; Who crowneth thee with lovingkindness and tender mercies;

5 Who satisfieth thy desire with good things, So that thy youth is renewed like the eagle.

6 Jehovah executeth righteous acts, And judgments for all that are oppressed.

7 He made known his ways unto Moses, His doings unto the children of Israel.

8 Jehovah is merciful and gracious, Slow to anger, and abundant in lovingkindness.

9 He will not always chide; Neither will he keep his anger for ever.

10 He hath not dealt with us after our sins, Nor rewarded us after our iniquities.

11 For as the heavens are high above the earth, So great is his lovingkindness toward them that fear him.

12 As far as the east is from the west, So far hath he removed our transgressions from us.

13   Like as a father pitieth his children, So Jehovah pitieth them that fear him.

14   For he knoweth our frame; He remembereth that we are dust.

15   As for man, his days are as grass; As a flower of the field, so he flourisheth.

16   For the wind passeth over it, and it is gone; And the place thereof shall know it no more.

17   But the lovingkindness of Jehovah is from everlasting to everlasting upon them that fear him, And his righteousness unto children's children;

18   To such as keep his covenant, And to those that remember his precepts to do them.

19   Jehovah hath established his throne in the heavens; And his kingdom ruleth over all.

20   Bless Jehovah, ye his angels, That are mighty in strength, that fulfil his word, Hearkening unto the voice of his word.

21   Bless Jehovah, all ye his hosts, Ye ministers of his, that do his pleasure.

22   Bless Jehovah, all ye his works, In all places of his dominion: Bless Jehovah, O my soul.

Psalm 104

1   Bless Jehovah, O my soul. O Jehovah my God, thou art very great; Thou
    art clothed with honor and majesty:

2   Who coverest thyself with light as with a garment; Who stretchest out
    the heavens like a curtain;

3   Who layeth the beams of his chambers in the waters; Who maketh the
    clouds his chariot; Who walketh upon the wings of the wind;

4   Who maketh winds his messengers; Flames of fire his ministers;

5   Who laid the foundations of the earth, That it should not be moved for
    ever.

6   Thou coveredst it with the deep as with a vesture; The waters stood above
    the mountains.

7   At thy rebuke they fled; At the voice of thy thunder they hasted away

8   (The mountains rose, the valleys sank down) Unto the place which thou
    hadst founded for them.

9   Thou hast set a bound that they may not pass over; That they turn not
    again to cover the earth.

10 He sendeth forth springs into the valleys; They run among the
    mountains;

11 They give drink to every beast of the field; The wild asses quench their
    thirst.

12 By them the birds of the heavens have their habitation; They sing among
    the branches.

13 He watereth the mountains from his chambers: The earth is filled with the fruit of thy works.

14 He causeth the grass to grow for the cattle, And herb for the service of man; That he may bring forth food out of the earth,

15 And wine that maketh glad the heart of man, And oil to make his face to shine, And bread that strengtheneth man's heart.

16 The trees of Jehovah are filled with moisture, The cedars of Lebanon, which he hath planted;

17 Where the birds make their nests: As for the stork, the fir-trees are her house.

18 The high mountains are for the wild goats; The rocks are a refuge for the conies.

19 He appointed the moon for seasons: The sun knoweth his going down.

20 Thou makest darkness, and it is night, Wherein all the beasts of the forest creep forth.

21 The young lions roar after their prey, And seek their food from God.

22 The sun ariseth, they get them away, And lay them down in their dens.

23 Man goeth forth unto his work And to his labor until the evening.

24 O Jehovah, how manifold are thy works! In wisdom hast thou made them all: The earth is full of thy riches.

25 Yonder is the sea, great and wide, Wherein are things creeping innumerable, Both small and great beasts.

26 There go the ships; There is leviathan, whom thou hast formed to play therein.

27 These wait all for thee, That thou mayest give them their food in due season.

28 Thou givest unto them, they gather; Thou openest thy hand, they are satisfied with good.

29 Thou hidest thy face, they are troubled; Thou takest away their breath, they die, And return to their dust.

30 Thou sendest forth thy Spirit, they are created; And thou renewest the face of the ground.

31 Let the glory of Jehovah endure for ever; Let Jehovah rejoice in his works:

32 Who looketh on the earth, and it trembleth; He toucheth the mountains, and they smoke.

33 I will sing unto Jehovah as long as I live: I will sing praise to my God while I have any being.

34 Let thy meditation be sweet unto him: I will rejoice in Jehovah.

35 Let sinners be consumed out of the earth. And let the wicked be no more. Bless Jehovah, O my soul. Praise ye Jehovah.

Psalm 105

1 Oh give thanks unto Jehovah, call upon his name; Make known among the peoples his doings.

2 Sing unto him, sing praises unto him; Talk ye of all his marvelous works.

3 Glory ye in his holy name: Let the heart of them rejoice that seek Jehovah.

4 Seek ye Jehovah and his strength; Seek his face evermore.

5 Remember his marvellous works that he hath done, His wonders, and the judgments of his mouth,

6 O ye seed of Abraham his servant, Ye children of Jacob, his chosen ones.

7 He is Jehovah our God: His judgments are in all the earth.

8 He hath remembered his covenant for ever, The word which he commanded to a thousand generations,

9 The covenant which he made with Abraham, And his oath unto Isaac,

10 And confirmed the same unto Jacob for a statute, To Israel for an everlasting covenant,

11 Saying, Unto thee will I give the land of Canaan, The lot of your inheritance;

12 When they were but a few men in number, Yea, very few, and sojourners in it.

13 And they went about from nation to nation, From one kingdom to another people.

14   He suffered no man to do them wrong; Yea, he reproved kings for their sakes,

15   Saying, Touch not mine anointed ones, And do my prophets no harm.

16   And he called for a famine upon the land; He brake the whole staff of bread.

17   He sent a man before them; Joseph was sold for a servant:

18   His feet they hurt with fetters: He was laid in chains of iron,

19   Until the time that his word came to pass, The word of Jehovah tried him.

20   The king sent and loosed him; Even the ruler of peoples, and let him go free.

21   He made him lord of his house, And ruler of all his substance;

22   To bind his princes at his pleasure, And teach his elders wisdom.

23   Israel also came into Egypt; And Jacob sojourned in the land of Ham.

24   And he increased his people greatly, And made them stronger than their adversaries.

25   He turned their heart to hate his people, To deal subtly with his servants.

26   He sent Moses his servant, And Aaron whom he had chosen.

27   They set among them his signs, And wonders in the land of Ham.

28   He sent darkness, and made it dark; And they rebelled not against his words.

29   He turned their waters into blood, And slew their fish.

30   Their land swarmed with frogs In the chambers of their kings.

31 He spake, and there came swarms of flies, And lice in all their borders.

32 He gave them hail for rain, And flaming fire in their land.

33 He smote their vines also and their fig-trees, And brake the trees of their borders.

34 He spake, and the locust came, And the grasshopper, and that without number,

35 And did eat up every herb in their land, And did eat up the fruit of their ground.

36 He smote also all the first-born in their land, The chief of all their strength.

37 And he brought them forth with silver and gold; And there was not one feeble person among his tribes.

38 Egypt was glad when they departed; For the fear of them had fallen upon them.

39 He spread a cloud for a covering, And fire to give light in the night.

40 They asked, and he brought quails, And satisfied them with the bread of heaven.

41 He opened the rock, and waters gushed out; They ran in the dry places like a river.

42 For he remembered his holy word, And Abraham his servant.

43 And he brought forth his people with joy, And his chosen with singing.

44 And he gave them the lands of the nations; And they took the labor of the peoples in possession:

45 That they might keep his statutes, And observe his laws. Praise ye Jehovah.

Psalm 106

1   Praise ye Jehovah. Oh give thanks unto Jehovah; for he is good; For his loving kindness endureth forever.

2   Who can utter the mighty acts of Jehovah, Or show forth all his praise?

3   Blessed are they that keep justice, And he that doeth righteousness at all times.

4   Remember me, O Jehovah, with the favor that thou bearest unto thy people; Oh visit me with thy salvation,

5   That I may see the prosperity of thy chosen, That I may rejoice in the gladness of thy nation, That I may glory with thine inheritance.

6   We have sinned with our fathers, We have committed iniquity, we have done wickedly.

7   Our fathers understood not thy wonders in Egypt; They remembered not the multitude of thy loving kindnesses, But were rebellious at the sea, even at the Red Sea.

8   Nevertheless he saved them for his name's sake, That he might make his mighty power to be known.

9   He rebuked the Red Sea also, and it was dried up: So he led them through the depths, as through a wilderness.

10   And he saved them from the hand of him that hated them, And redeemed them from the hand of the enemy.

11   And the waters covered their adversaries; There was not one of them left.

12   Then believed they his words; They sang his praise.

13   They soon forgat his works; They waited not for his counsel,

14   But lusted exceedingly in the wilderness, And tempted God in the desert.

15   And he gave them their request, But sent leanness into their soul.

16   They envied Moses also in the camp, And Aaron the saint of Jehovah.

17   The earth opened and swallowed up Dathan, And covered the company of Abiram.

18   And a fire was kindled in their company; The flame burned up the wicked.

19   They made a calf in Horeb, And worshipped a molten image.

20   Thus they changed their glory For the likeness of an ox that eateth grass.

21   They forgat God their Saviour, Who had done great things in Egypt,

22   Wondrous works in the land of Ham, And terrible things by the Red Sea.

23   Therefore he said that he would destroy them, Had not Moses his chosen stood before him in the breach, To turn away his wrath, lest he should destroy them.

24   Yea, they despised the pleasant land, They believed not his word,

25   But murmured in their tents, And hearkened not unto the voice of Jehovah.

26   Therefore he sware unto them, That he would overthrow them in the wilderness,

27   And that he would overthrow their seed among the nations, And scatter them in the lands.

28   They joined themselves also unto Baal-peor, And ate the sacrifices of the dead.

29   Thus they provoked him to anger with their doings; And the plague brake in upon them.

30   Then stood up Phinehas, and executed judgment; And so the plague was stayed.

31   And that was reckoned unto him for righteousness, Unto all generations for evermore.

32   They angered him also at the waters of Meribah, So that it went ill with Moses for their sakes;

33   Because they were rebellious against his spirit, And he spake unadvisedly with his lips.

34   They did not destroy the peoples, As Jehovah commanded them,

35   But mingled themselves with the nations, And learned their works,

36   And served their idols, Which became a snare unto them.

37   Yea, they sacrificed their sons and their daughters unto demons,

38   And shed innocent blood, Even the blood of their sons and of their daughters, Whom they sacrificed unto the idols of Canaan; And the land was polluted with blood.

39   Thus were they defiled with their works, And played the harlot in their doings.

40   Therefore was the wrath of Jehovah kindled against his people, And he abhorred his inheritance.

41   And he gave them into the hand of the nations; And they that hated them ruled over them.

42 Their enemies also oppressed them, And they were brought into subjection under their hand.

43 Many times did he deliver them; But they were rebellious in their counsel, And were brought low in their iniquity.

44 Nevertheless he regarded their distress, When he heard their cry:

45 And he remembered for them his covenant, And repented according to the multitude of his lovingkindnesses.

46 He made them also to be pitied Of all those that carried them captive.

47 Save us, O Jehovah our God, And gather us from among the nations, To give thanks unto thy holy name, And to triumph in thy praise.

48 Blessed be Jehovah, the God of Israel, From everlasting even to everlasting. And let all the people say, Amen. Praise ye Jehovah.

Psalm 107

1   O give thanks unto Jehovah; For he is good; For his lovingkindness
    endureth for ever.

2   Let the redeemed of Jehovah say so, Whom he hath redeemed from the
    hand of the adversary,

3   And gathered out of the lands, From the east and from the west, From
    the north and from the south.

4   They wandered in the wilderness in a desert way; They found no city of
    habitation.

5   Hungry and thirsty, Their soul fainted in them.

6   Then they cried unto Jehovah in their trouble, And he delivered them
    out of their distresses,

7   He led them also by a straight way, That they might go to a city of
    habitation.

8   Oh that men would praise Jehovah for his lovingkindness, And for his
    wonderful works to the children of men!

9   For he satisfieth the longing soul, And the hungry soul he filleth with
    good.

10 Such as sat in darkness and in the shadow of death, Being bound in
    affliction and iron,

11 Because they rebelled against the words of God, And contemned the
    counsel of the Most High:

12 Therefore he brought down their heart with labor; They fell down, and
    there was none to help.

13   Then they cried unto Jehovah in their trouble, And he saved them out of their distresses.

14   He brought them out of darkness and the shadow of death, And brake their bonds in sunder.

15   Oh that men would praise Jehovah for his lovingkindness, And for his wonderful works to the children of men!

16   For he hath broken the gates of brass, And cut the bars of iron in sunder.

17   Fools because of their transgression, And because of their iniquities, are afflicted.

18   Their soul abhorreth all manner of food; And they draw near unto the gates of death.

19   Then they cry unto Jehovah in their trouble, And he saveth them out of their distresses.

20   He sendeth his word, and healeth them, And delivereth them from their destructions.

21   Oh that men would praise Jehovah for his lovingkindness, And for his wonderful works to the children of men!

22   And let them offer the sacrifices of thanksgiving, And declare his works with singing.

23   They that go down to the sea in ships, That do business in great waters;

24   These see the works of Jehovah, And his wonders in the deep.

25   For he commandeth, and raiseth the stormy wind, Which lifteth up the waves thereof.

26   They mount up to the heavens, they go down again to the depths: Their soul melteth away because of trouble.

²⁷ They reel to and fro, and stagger like a drunken man, And are at their wits' end.

²⁸ Then they cry unto Jehovah in their trouble, And he bringeth them out of their distresses.

²⁹ He maketh the storm a calm, So that the waves thereof are still.

³⁰ Then are they glad because they are quiet; So he bringeth them unto their desired haven.

³¹ Oh that men would praise Jehovah for his lovingkindness, And for his wonderful works to the children of men!

³² Let them exalt him also in the assembly of the people, And praise him in the seat of the elders.

³³ He turneth rivers into a wilderness, And watersprings into a thirsty ground;

³⁴ A fruitful land into a salt desert, For the wickedness of them that dwell therein.

³⁵ He turneth a wilderness into a pool of water, And a dry land into watersprings.

³⁶ And there he maketh the hungry to dwell, That they may prepare a city of habitation,

³⁷ And sow fields, and plant vineyards, And get them fruits of increase.

³⁸ He blesseth them also, so that they are multiplied greatly; And he suffereth not their cattle to decrease.

³⁹ Again, they are diminished and bowed down Through oppression, trouble, and sorrow.

⁴⁰ He poureth contempt upon princes, And causeth them to wander in the waste, where there is no way.

41 Yet setteth he the needy on high from affliction, And maketh him families like a flock.

42 The upright shall see it, and be glad; And all iniquity shall stop her mouth.

43 Whoso is wise will give heed to these things; And they will consider the lovingkindnesses of Jehovah. Psalm 108 A Song, A Psalm of David.

Psalm 108

1   My heart is fixed, O God; I will sing, yea, I will sing praises, even with my glory.

2   Awake, psaltery and harp: I myself will awake right early.

3   I will give thanks unto thee, O Jehovah, among the peoples; And I will sing praises unto thee among the nations.

4   For thy lovingkindness is great above the heavens; And thy truth reacheth unto the skies.

5   Be thou exalted, O God, above the heavens, And thy glory above all the earth.

6   That thy beloved may be delivered, Save with thy right hand, and answer us.

7   God hath spoken in his holiness: I will exult; I will divide Shechem, and mete out the valley of Succoth.

8   Gilead is mine; Manasseh is mine; Ephraim also is the defence of my head; Judah is my sceptre.

9   Moab is my washpot; Upon Edom will I cast my shoe; Over Philistia will I shout.

10 Who will bring me into the fortified city? Who hath led me unto Edom?

11 Hast not thou cast us off, O God? And thou goest not forth, O God, with our hosts.

12 Give us help against the adversary; For vain is the help of man.

13 Through God we shall do valiantly: For he it is that will tread down our adversaries.

Psalm 109

For the Chief Musician. A Psalm of David.

1   Hold not thy peace, O God of my praise;

2   For the mouth of the wicked and the mouth of deceit have they opened against me: They have spoken unto me with a lying tongue.

3   They have compassed me about also with words of hatred, And fought against me without a cause.

4   For my love they are my adversaries: But I give myself unto prayer.

5   And they have rewarded me evil for good, And hatred for my love.

6   Set thou a wicked man over him; And let an adversary stand at his right hand.

7   When he is judged, let him come forth guilty; And let his prayer be turned into sin.

8   Let his days be few; And let another take his office.

9   Let his children be fatherless, And his wife a widow.

10   Let his children be vagabonds, and beg; And let them seek their bread out of their desolate places.

11   Let the extortioner catch all that he hath; And let strangers make spoil of his labor.

12   Let there be none to extend kindness unto him; Neither let there be any to have pity on his fatherless children.

13   Let his posterity be cut off; In the generation following let their name be blotted out.

14   Let the iniquity of his fathers be remembered with Jehovah; And let not the sin of his mother be blotted out.

15   Let them be before Jehovah continually, That he may cut off the memory of them from the earth;

16   Because he remembered not to show kindness, But persecuted the poor and needy man, And the broken in heart, to slay them.   `

17   Yea, he loved cursing, and it came unto him; And he delighted not in blessing, and it was far from him.

18   He clothed himself also with cursing as with his garment, And it came into his inward parts like water, And like oil into his bones.

19   Let it be unto him as the raiment wherewith he covereth himself, And for the girdle wherewith he is girded continually.

20   This is the reward of mine adversaries from Jehovah, And of them that speak evil against my soul.

21   But deal thou with me, O Jehovah the Lord, for thy name's sake: Because thy lovingkindness is good, deliver thou me;

22   For I am poor and needy, And my heart is wounded within me.

23   I am gone like the shadow when it declineth: I am tossed up and down as the locust.

24   My knees are weak through fasting; And my flesh faileth of fatness.

25   I am become also a reproach unto them: When they see me, they shake their head.

26   Help me, O Jehovah my God; Oh save me according to thy lovingkindness:

27   That they may know that this is thy hand; That thou, Jehovah, hast done it.

28   Let them curse, but bless thou: When they arise, they shall be put to shame, But thy servant shall rejoice.

29   Let mine adversaries be clothed with dishonor, And let them cover themselves with their own shame as with a robe.

30   I will give great thanks unto Jehovah with my mouth; Yea, I will praise him among the multitude.

31   For he will stand at the right hand of the needy, To save him from them that judge his soul.

Psalm 110

A Psalm of David.

1   Jehovah saith unto my Lord, Sit thou at my right hand, Until I make thine enemies thy footstool.

2   Jehovah will send forth the rod of thy strength out of Zion: Rule thou in the midst of thine enemies.

3   Thy people offer themselves willingly In the day of thy power, in holy array: Out of the womb of the morning Thou hast the dew of thy youth.

4   Jehovah hath sworn, and will not repent: Thou art a priest for ever After the order of Melchizedek.

5   The Lord at thy right hand Will strike through kings in the day of his wrath.

6   He will judge among the nations, He will fill the places with dead bodies; He will strike through the head in many countries.

7   He will drink of the brook in the way: Therefore will he lift up the head.

Psalm 111

1   Praise ye Jehovah. I will give thanks unto Jehovah with my whole heart, In the council of the upright, and in the congregation.

2   The works of Jehovah are great, Sought out of all them that have pleasure therein.

3   His work is honor and majesty; And his righteousness endureth for ever.

4   He hath made his wonderful works to be remembered: Jehovah is gracious and merciful.

5   He hath given food unto them that fear him: He will ever be mindful of his covenant.

6   He hath showed his people the power of his works, In giving them the heritage of the nations.

7   The works of his hands are truth and justice; All his precepts are sure.

8   They are established for ever and ever; They are done in truth and uprightness.

9   He hath sent redemption unto his people; He hath commanded his covenant for ever: Holy and reverend is his name.

10 The fear of Jehovah is the beginning of wisdom; A good understanding have all they that do his commandments: His praise endureth for ever.

Psalm 112

1 Praise ye Jehovah. Blessed is the man that feareth Jehovah, That delighteth greatly in his commandments.

2 His seed shall be mighty upon earth: The generation of the upright shall be blessed.

3 Wealth and riches are in his house; And his righteousness endureth for ever.

4 Unto the upright there ariseth light in the darkness: He is gracious, and merciful, and righteous.

5 Well is it with the man that dealeth graciously and lendeth; He shall maintain his cause in judgment.

6 For he shall never be moved; The righteous shall be had in everlasting remembrance.

7 He shall not be afraid of evil tidings: His heart is fixed, trusting in Jehovah.

8 His heart is established, he shall not be afraid, Until he see his desire upon his adversaries.

9 He hath dispersed, he hath given to the needy; His righteousness endureth for ever: His horn shall be exalted with honor.

10 The wicked shall see it, and be grieved; He shall gnash with his teeth, and melt away: The desire of the wicked shall perish.

Psalm 113

1   Praise ye Jehovah. Praise, O ye servants of Jehovah, Praise the name of Jehovah.

2   Blessed be the name of Jehovah From this time forth and for evermore.

3   From the rising of the sun unto the going down of the same Jehovah's name is to be praised.

4   Jehovah is high above all nations, And his glory above the heavens.

5   Who is like unto Jehovah our God, That hath his seat on high,

6   That humbleth himself to behold The things that are in heaven and in the earth?

7   He raiseth up the poor out of the dust, And lifteth up the needy from the dunghill;

8   That he may set him with princes, Even with the princes of his people.

9   He maketh the barren woman to keep house, And to be a joyful mother of children. Praise ye Jehovah.

Psalm 114

1 When Israel went forth out of Egypt, The house of Jacob from a people of strange language;

2 Judah became his sanctuary, Israel his dominion.

3 The sea saw it, and fled; The Jordan was driven back.

4 The mountains skipped like rams, The little hills like lambs.

5 What aileth thee, O thou sea, that thou fleest? Thou Jordan, that thou turnest back?

6 Ye mountains, that ye skip like rams; Ye little hills, like lambs?

7 Tremble, thou earth, at the presence of the Lord, At the presence of the God of Jacob,

8 Who turned the rock into a pool of water, The flint into a fountain of waters.

Psalm 115

1 Not unto us, O Jehovah, not unto us, But unto thy name give glory, For thy loving kindness, and for thy truth's sake.

2 Wherefore should the nations say, Where is now their God?

3 But our God is in the heavens: He hath done whatsoever he pleased.

4 Their idols are silver and gold, The work of men's hands.

5 They have mouths, but they speak not; Eyes have they, but they see not;

6 They have ears, but they hear not; Noses have they, but they smell not;

7 They have hands, but they handle not; Feet have they, but they walk not; Neither speak they through their throat.

8 They that make them shall be like unto them; Yea, every one that trusteth in them.

9 O Israel, trust thou in Jehovah: He is their help and their shield.

10 O house of Aaron, trust ye in Jehovah: He is their help and their shield.

11 Ye that fear Jehovah, trust in Jehovah: He is their help and their shield.

12 Jehovah hath been mindful of us; he will bless us: He will bless the house of Israel; He will bless the house of Aaron.

13 He will bless them that fear Jehovah, Both small and great.

14 Jehovah increase you more and more, You and your children.

15   Blessed are ye of Jehovah, Who made heaven and earth.

16   The heavens are the heavens of Jehovah; But the earth hath he given to the children of men.

17   The dead praise not Jehovah, Neither any that go down into silence;

18   But we will bless Jehovah From this time forth and for evermore. Praise ye Jehovah.

Psalm 116

1 I love Jehovah, because he heareth My voice and my supplications.

2 Because he hath inclined his ear unto me, Therefore will I call upon him as long as I live.

3 The cords of death compassed me, And the pains of Sheol gat hold upon me: I found trouble and sorrow.

4 Then called I upon the name of Jehovah: O Jehovah, I beseech thee, deliver my soul.

5 Gracious is Jehovah, and righteous; Yea, our God is merciful.

6 Jehovah preserveth the simple: I was brought low, and he saved me.

7 Return unto thy rest, O my soul; For Jehovah hath dealt bountifully with thee.

8 For thou hast delivered my soul from death, Mine eyes from tears, And my feet from falling.

9 I will walk before Jehovah In the land of the living.

10 I believe, for I will speak: I was greatly afflicted:

11 I said in my haste, All men are liars.

12 What shall I render unto Jehovah For all his benefits toward me?

13 I will take the cup of salvation, And call upon the name of Jehovah.

14 I will pay my vows unto Jehovah, Yea, in the presence of all his people.

15 Precious in the sight of Jehovah Is the death of his saints.

16 O Jehovah, truly I am thy servant: I am thy servant, the son of thy handmaid; Thou hast loosed my bonds.

17 I will offer to thee the sacrifice of thanksgiving, And will call upon the name of Jehovah.

18 I will pay my vows unto Jehovah, Yea, in the presence of all his people,

19 In the courts of Jehovah's house, In the midst of thee, O Jerusalem. Praise ye Jehovah.

Psalm 117

1   O praise Jehovah, all ye nations; Laud him, all ye peoples.

2   For his lovingkindness is great toward us; And the truth of Jehovah endureth for ever. Praise ye Jehovah. Psalm 118

Psalm 118

1   Oh give thanks unto Jehovah; for he is good; For his lovingkindness endureth for ever.

2   Let Israel now say, That his lovingkindness endureth for ever.

3   Let the house of Aaron now say, That his lovingkindness endureth for ever.

4   Let them now that fear Jehovah say, That his lovingkindness endureth for ever.

5   Out of my distress I called upon Jehovah: Jehovah answered me and set me in a large place.

6   Jehovah is on my side; I will not fear: What can man do unto me?

7   Jehovah is on my side among them that help me: Therefore shall I see my desire upon them that hate me.

8   It is better to take refuge in Jehovah Than to put confidence in man.

9   It is better to take refuge in Jehovah Than to put confidence in princes.

10   All nations compassed me about: In the name of Jehovah I will cut them off.

11   They compassed me about; yea, they compassed me about: In the name of Jehovah I will cut them off.

12   They compassed me about like bees; They are quenched as the fire of thorns: In the name of Jehovah I will cut them off.

13   Thou didst thrust sore at me that I might fall; But Jehovah helped me.

14   Jehovah is my strength and song; And he is become my salvation.

15 The voice of rejoicing and salvation is in the tents of the righteous: The right hand of Jehovah doeth valiantly.

16 The right hand of Jehovah is exalted: The right hand of Jehovah doeth valiantly.

17 I shall not die, but live, And declare the works of Jehovah.

18 Jehovah hath chastened me sore; But he hath not given me over unto death.

19 Open to me the gates of righteousness: I will enter into them, I will give thanks unto Jehovah.

20 This is the gate of Jehovah; The righteous shall enter into it.

21 I will give thanks unto thee; for thou hast answered me, And art become my salvation.

22 The stone which the builders rejected Is become the head of the corner.

23 This is Jehovah's doing; It is marvellous in our eyes.

24 This is the day which Jehovah hath made; We will rejoice and be glad in it.

25 Save now, we beseech thee, O Jehovah: O Jehovah, we beseech thee, send now prosperity.

26 Blessed be he that cometh in the name of Jehovah: We have blessed you out of the house of Jehovah.

27 Jehovah is God, and he hath given us light: Bind the sacrifice with cords, even unto the horns of the altar.

28 Thou art my God, and I will give thanks unto thee: Thou art my God, I will exalt thee.

29 Oh give thanks unto Jehovah; for he is good; For his loving kindness endureth for ever.

Psalm 119

ALEPH.

1   Blessed are they that are perfect in the way, Who walk in the law of Jehovah.

2   Blessed are they that keep his testimonies, That seek him with the whole heart.

3   Yea, they do no unrighteousness; They walk in his ways.

4   Thou hast commanded us thy precepts, That we should observe them diligently.

5   Oh that my ways were established To observe thy statutes!

6   Then shall I not be put to shame, When I have respect unto all thy commandments.

7   I will give thanks unto thee with uprightness of heart, When I learn thy righteous judgments.

8   I will observe thy statutes: Oh forsake me not utterly.

BETH.

9   Wherewith shall a young man cleanse his way? By taking heed thereto according to thy word.

10   With my whole heart have I sought thee: Oh let me not wander from thy commandments.

11   Thy word have I laid up in my heart, That I might not sin against thee.

12   Blessed art thou, O Jehovah: Teach me thy statutes.

13 With my lips have I declared All the ordinances of thy mouth.

14 I have rejoiced in the way of thy testimonies, As much as in all riches.

15 I will meditate on thy precepts, And have respect unto thy ways.

16 I will delight myself in thy statutes: I will not forget thy word.

GIMEL.

17 Deal bountifully with thy servant, that I may live; So will I observe thy word.

18 Open thou mine eyes, that I may behold Wondrous things out of thy law.

19 I am a sojourner in the earth: Hide not thy commandments from me.

20 My soul breaketh for the longing That it hath unto thine ordinances at all times.

21 Thou hast rebuked the proud that are cursed, That do wander from thy commandments.

22 Take away from me reproach and contempt; For I have kept thy testimonies.

23 Princes also sat and talked against me; But thy servant did meditate on thy statutes.

24 Thy testimonies also are my delight And my counsellors.

DALETH.

25 My soul cleaveth unto the dust: Quicken thou me according to thy word.

26 I declared my ways, and thou answeredst me: Teach me thy statutes.

27 Make me to understand the way of thy precepts: So shall I meditate on thy wondrous works.

28 My soul melteth for heaviness: Strengthen thou me according unto thy word.

29 Remove from me the way of falsehood; And grant me thy law graciously.

30 I have chosen the way of faithfulness: Thine ordinances have I set before me.

31 I cleave unto thy testimonies: O Jehovah, put me not to shame.

32 I will run the way of thy commandments, When thou shalt enlarge my heart.

HE.

33 Teach me, O Jehovah, the way of thy statutes; And I shall keep it unto the end.

34 Give me understanding, and I shall keep thy law; Yea, I shall observe it with my whole heart.

35 Make me to go in the path of thy commandments; For therein do I delight.

36 Incline my heart unto thy testimonies, And not to covetousness.

37 Turn away mine eyes from beholding vanity, And quicken me in thy ways.

38 Confirm unto thy servant thy word, Which is in order unto the fear of thee.

39 Turn away my reproach whereof I am afraid; For thine ordinances are good.

40 Behold, I have longed after thy precepts: Quicken me in thy righteousness.

VAV.

41 Let thy lovingkindnesses also come unto me, O Jehovah, Even thy salvation, according to thy word.

42 So shall I have an answer for him that reproacheth me; For I trust in thy word.

43 And take not the word of truth utterly out of my mouth; For I have hoped in thine ordinances.

44 So shall I observe thy law continually For ever and ever.

45 And I shall walk at liberty; For I have sought thy precepts.

46 I will also speak of thy testimonies before kings, And shall not be put to shame.

47 And I will delight myself in thy commandments, Which I have loved.

48 I will lift up my hands also unto thy commandments, which I have loved; And I will meditate on thy statutes.

ZAYIN.

49 Remember the word unto thy servant, Because thou hast made me to hope.

50 This is my comfort in my affliction; For thy word hath quickened me.

51 The proud have had me greatly in derision: Yet have I not swerved from thy law.

52 I have remembered thine ordinances of old, O Jehovah, And have comforted myself.

53 Hot indignation hath taken hold upon me, Because of the wicked that forsake thy law.

54   Thy statutes have been my songs In the house of my pilgrimage.

55   I have remembered thy name, O Jehovah, in the night, And have observed thy law.

56   This I have had, Because I have kept thy precepts.

HHETH.

57   Jehovah is my portion: I have said that I would observe thy words.

58   I entreated thy favor with my whole heart: Be merciful unto me according to thy word.

59   I thought on my ways, And turned my feet unto thy testimonies.

60   I made haste, and delayed not, To observe thy commandments.

61   The cords of the wicked have wrapped me round; But I have not forgotten thy law.

62   At midnight I will rise to give thanks unto thee Because of thy righteous ordinances.

63   I am a companion of all them that fear thee, And of them that observe thy precepts.

64   The earth, O Jehovah, is full of thy lovingkindness: Teach me thy statutes.

TETH.

65   Thou hast dealt well with thy servant, O Jehovah, according unto thy word.

66   Teach me good judgment and knowledge; For I have believed in thy commandments.

67   Before I was afflicted I went astray; But now I observe thy word.

68 Thou art good, and doest good; Teach me thy statutes.

69 The proud have forged a lie against me: With my whole heart will I keep thy precepts.

70 Their heart is as fat as grease; But I delight in thy law.

71 It is good for me that I have been afflicted; That I may learn thy statutes.

72 The law of thy mouth is better unto me Than thousands of gold and silver.

YODH.

73 Thy hands have made me and fashioned me: Give me understanding, that I may learn thy commandments.

74 They that fear thee shall see me and be glad, Because I have hoped in thy word.

75 I know, O Jehovah, that thy judgments are righteous, And that in faithfulness thou hast afflicted me.

76 Let, I pray thee, thy lovingkindness be for my comfort, According to thy word unto thy servant.

77 Let thy tender mercies come unto me, that I may live; For thy law is my delight.

78 Let the proud be put to shame; For they have overthrown me wrongfully: But I will meditate on thy precepts.

79 Let those that fear thee turn unto me; And they shall know thy testimonies.

80 Let my heart be perfect in thy statutes, That I be not put to shame.

KAPH.

81 My soul fainteth for thy salvation; But I hope in thy word.

82 Mine eyes fail for thy word, While I say, When wilt thou comfort me?

83   For I am become like a wine-skin in the smoke; Yet do I not forget thy statutes.

84   How many are the days of thy servant? When wilt thou execute judgment on them that persecute me?

85   The proud have digged pits for me, Who are not according to thy law.

86   All thy commandments are faithful: They persecute me wrongfully; help thou me.

87   They had almost consumed me upon earth; But I forsook not thy precepts.

LAMEDH.

88   Quicken me after thy lovingkindness; So shall I observe the testimony of thy mouth.

89   For ever, O Jehovah, Thy word is settled in heaven.

90   Thy faithfulness is unto all generations: Thou hast established the earth, and it abideth.

91   They abide this day according to thine ordinances; For all things are thy servants.

92   Unless thy law had been my delight, I should then have perished in mine affliction.

93   I will never forget thy precepts; For with them thou hast quickened me.

94   I am thine, save me; For I have sought thy precepts.

95   The wicked have waited for me, to destroy me; But I will consider thy testimonies.

MEM.

96 I have seen an end of all perfection; But thy commandment is exceeding broad.

97 Oh how love I thy law! It is my meditation all the day.

98 Thy commandments make me wiser than mine enemies; For they are ever with me.

99 I have more understanding than all my teachers; For thy testimonies are my meditation.

100 I understand more than the aged, Because I have kept thy precepts.

101 I have refrained my feet from every evil way, That I might observe thy word.

102 I have not turned aside from thine ordinances; For thou hast taught me.

103 How sweet are thy words unto my taste! Yea, sweeter than honey to my mouth!

104 Through thy precepts I get understanding: Therefore I hate every false way.

NUN.

105 Thy word is a lamp unto my feet, And light unto my path.

106 I have sworn, and have confirmed it, That I will observe thy righteous ordinances.

107 I am afflicted very much: Quicken me, O Jehovah, according unto thy word.

108 Accept, I beseech thee, the freewill-offerings of my mouth, O Jehovah, And teach me thine ordinances.

109   My soul is continually in my hand; Yet do I not forget thy law.

110   The wicked have laid a snare for me; Yet have I not gone astray from thy precepts.

111   Thy testimonies have I taken as a heritage for ever; For they are the rejoicing of my heart.

112   I have inclined my heart to perform thy statutes For ever, even unto the end.

SAMEKH.

113   I hate them that are of a double mind; But thy law do I love.

114   Thou art my hiding-place and my shield: I hope in thy word.

115   Depart from me, ye evil-doers, That I may keep the commandments of my God.

116   Uphold me according unto thy word, that I may live; And let me not be ashamed of my hope.

117   Hold thou me up, and I shall be safe, And shall have respect unto thy statutes continually.

118   Thou hast set at nought all them that err from thy statutes; For their deceit is falsehood.

119   Thou puttest away all the wicked of the earth like dross: Therefore I love thy testimonies.

120   My flesh trembleth for fear of thee; And I am afraid of thy judgments.

AYIN.

121   I have done justice and righteousness: Leave me not to mine oppressors.

122   Be surety for thy servant for good: Let not the proud oppress me.

123 Mine eyes fail for thy salvation, And for thy righteous word.

124 Deal with thy servant according unto thy lovingkindness, And teach me thy statutes.

125 I am thy servant; give me understanding, That I may know thy testimonies.

126 It is time for Jehovah to work; For they have made void thy law.

127 Therefore I love thy commandments Above gold, yea, above fine gold.

128 Therefore I esteem all thy precepts concerning all things to be right; And I hate every false way.

PE.

129 Thy testimonies are wonderful; Therefore doth my soul keep them.

130 The opening of thy words giveth light; It giveth understanding unto the simple.

131 I opened wide my mouth, and panted; For I longed for thy commandments.

132 Turn thee unto me, and have mercy upon me, As thou usest to do unto those that love thy name.

133 Establish my footsteps in thy word; And let not any iniquity have dominion over me.

134 Redeem me from the oppression of man: So will I observe thy precepts.

135 Make thy face to shine upon thy servant; And teach me thy statutes.

136 Streams of water run down mine eyes, Because they observe not thy law.

TSADHE.

137 Righteous art thou, O Jehovah, And upright are thy judgments.

138 Thou hast commanded thy testimonies in righteousness And very faithfulness.

139 My zeal hath consumed me, Because mine adversaries have forgotten thy words.

140 Thy word is very pure; Therefore thy servant loveth it.

141 I am small and despised; Yet do I not forget thy precepts.

142 Thy righteousness is an everlasting righteousness, And thy law is truth.

143 Trouble and anguish have taken hold on me; Yet thy commandments are my delight.

144 Thy testimonies are righteous for ever: Give me understanding, and I shall live.

QOPH.

145 I have called with my whole heart; answer me, O Jehovah: I will keep thy statutes.

146 I have called unto thee; save me, And I shall observe thy testimonies.

147 I anticipated the dawning of the morning, and cried: I hoped in thy words.

148 Mine eyes anticipated the night-watches, That I might meditate on thy word.

149 Hear my voice according unto thy lovingkindness: Quicken me, O Jehovah, according to thine ordinances.

150 They draw nigh that follow after wickedness; They are far from thy law.

151 Thou art nigh, O Jehovah; And all thy commandments are truth.

152 Of old have I known from thy testimonies, That thou hast founded them for ever.

RESH.

153 Consider mine affliction, and deliver me; For I do not forget thy law.

154 Plead thou my cause, and redeem me: Quicken me according to thy word.

155 Salvation is far from the wicked; For they seek not thy statutes.

156 Great are thy tender mercies, O Jehovah: Quicken me according to thine ordinances.

157 Many are my persecutors and mine adversaries; Yet have I not swerved from thy testimonies.

158 I beheld the treacherous, and was grieved, Because they observe not thy word.

159 Consider how I love thy precepts: Quicken me, O Jehovah, according to thy lovingkindness.

160 The sum of thy word is truth; And every one of thy righteous ordinances endureth for ever.

SHIN.

161 Princes have persecuted me without a cause; But my heart standeth in awe of thy words.

162 I rejoice at thy word, As one that findeth great spoil.

163 I hate and abhor falsehood; But thy law do I love.

164 Seven times a day do I praise thee, Because of thy righteous ordinances.

165 Great peace have they that love thy law; And they have no occasion of stumbling.

166 I have hoped for thy salvation, O Jehovah, And have done thy commandments.

167 My soul hath observed thy testimonies; And I love them exceedingly.

168 I have observed thy precepts and thy testimonies; For all my ways are before thee.

TAV.

169 Let my cry come near before thee, O Jehovah: Give me understanding according to thy word.

170 Let my supplication come before thee: Deliver me according to thy word.

171 Let my lips utter praise; For thou teachest me thy statutes.

172 Let my tongue sing of thy word; For all thy commandments are righteousness.

173 Let thy hand be ready to help me; For I have chosen thy precepts.

174 I have longed for thy salvation, O Jehovah; And thy law is my delight.

175 Let my soul live, and it shall praise thee; And let thine ordinances help me.

176 I have gone astray like a lost sheep; Seek thy servant; For I do not forget thy commandments.

Psalm 120

A Song of Ascents.

1 In my distress I cried unto Jehovah, And he answered me.

2 Deliver my soul, O Jehovah, from lying lips, And from a deceitful tongue.

3 What shall be given unto thee, and what shall be done more unto thee, Thou deceitful tongue?

4 Sharp arrows of the mighty, With coals of juniper.

5 Woe is me, that I sojourn in Meshech, That I dwell among the tents of Kedar!

6 My soul hath long had her dwelling With him that hateth peace.

7 I am for peace: But when I speak, they are for war.

Psalm 121

A Song of Ascents.

1   I will lift up mine eyes unto the mountains: From whence shall my help come?

2   My help cometh from Jehovah, Who made heaven and earth.

3   He will not suffer thy foot to be moved: He that keepeth thee will not slumber.

4   Behold, he that keepeth Israel Will neither slumber nor sleep.

5   Jehovah is thy keeper: Jehovah is thy shade upon thy right hand.

6   The sun shall not smite thee by day, Nor the moon by night.

7   Jehovah will keep thee from all evil; He will keep thy soul.

8   Jehovah will keep thy going out and thy coming in From this time forth and for evermore.

Psalm 122

A Song of Ascents; of David.

1   I was glad when they said unto me, Let us go unto the house of Jehovah.

2   Our feet are standing Within thy gates, O Jerusalem,

3   Jerusalem, that art builded As a city that is compact together;

4   Whither the tribes go up, even the tribes of Jehovah, For an ordinance for Israel, To give thanks unto the name of Jehovah.

5   For there are set thrones for judgment, The thrones of the house of David.

6   Pray for the peace of Jerusalem: They shall prosper that love thee.

7   Peace be within thy walls, And prosperity within thy palaces.

8   For my brethren and companions' sakes, I will now say, Peace be within thee.

9   For the sake of the house of Jehovah our God I will seek thy good.

Psalm 123

A Song of Ascents.

1   Unto thee do I lift up mine eyes, O thou that sittest in the heavens.

2   Behold, as the eyes of servants look unto the hand of their master, As the eyes of a maid unto the hand of her mistress; So our eyes look unto Jehovah our God, Until he have mercy upon us.

3   Have mercy upon us, O Jehovah, have mercy upon us; For we are exceedingly filled with contempt.

4   Our soul is exceedingly filled With the scoffing of those that are at ease, And with the contempt of the proud.

Psalm 124

A Song of Ascents; of David.

1   If it had not been Jehovah who was on our side, Let Israel now say,

2   If it had not been Jehovah who was on our side, When men rose up against us;

3   Then they had swallowed us up alive, When their wrath was kindled against us;

4   Then the waters had overwhelmed us, The stream had gone over our soul;

5   Then the proud waters had gone over our soul.

6   Blessed be Jehovah, Who hath not given us as a prey to their teeth.

7   Our soul is escaped as a bird out of the snare of the fowlers: The snare is broken, and we are escaped.

8   Our help is in the name of Jehovah, Who made heaven and earth.

Psalm 125

A Song of Ascents.

1 They that trust in Jehovah Are as mount Zion, which cannot be moved, but abideth for ever.

2 As the mountains are round about Jerusalem, So Jehovah is round about his people From this time forth and for evermore.

3 For the sceptre of wickedness shall not rest upon the lot of the righteous; That the righteous put not forth their hands unto iniquity.

4 Do good, O Jehovah, unto those that are good, And to them that are upright in their hearts.

5 But as for such as turn aside unto their crooked ways, Jehovah will lead them forth with the workers of iniquity. Peace be upon Israel.

Psalm 126

A Song of Ascents.

1   When Jehovah brought back those that returned to Zion, We were like unto them that dream.

2   Then was our mouth filled with laughter, And our tongue with singing: Then said they among the nations, Jehovah hath done great things for them.

3   Jehovah hath done great things for us, Whereof we are glad.

4   Turn again our captivity, O Jehovah, As the streams in the South.

5   They that sow in tears shall reap in joy.

6   He that goeth forth and weepeth, bearing seed for sowing, Shall doubtless come again with joy, bringing his sheaves with him.

Psalm 127

A Song of Ascents; of Solomon.

1 Except Jehovah build the house, They labor in vain that build it: Except Jehovah keep the city, The watchman waketh but in vain.

2 It is vain for you to rise up early, To take rest late, To eat the bread of toil; For so he giveth unto his beloved sleep.

3 Lo, children are a heritage of Jehovah; And the fruit of the womb is his reward.

4 As arrows in the hand of a mighty man, So are the children of youth.

5 Happy is the man that hath his quiver full of them: They shall not be put to shame, When they speak with their enemies in the gate.

Psalm 128

A Song of Ascents.

1   Blessed is every one that feareth Jehovah, That walketh in his ways.

2   For thou shalt eat the labor of thy hands: Happy shalt thou be, and it shall be well with thee.

3   Thy wife shall be as a fruitful vine, In the innermost parts of thy house; Thy children like olive plants, Round about thy table.

4   Behold, thus shall the man be blessed That feareth Jehovah.

5   Jehovah bless thee out of Zion: And see thou the good of Jerusalem all the days of thy life.

6   Yea, see thou thy children's children. Peace be upon Israel.

Psalm 129

A Song of Ascents

1 Many a time have they afflicted me from my youth up, Let Israel now say,

2 Many a time have they afflicted me from my youth up: Yet they have not prevailed against me.

3 The plowers plowed upon my back; They made long their furrows.

4 Jehovah is righteous: He hath cut asunder the cords of the wicked.

5 Let them be put to shame and turned backward, All they that hate Zion.

6 Let them be as the grass upon the housetops, Which withereth before it groweth up;

7 Wherewith the reaper filleth not his hand, Nor he that bindeth sheaves his bosom.

8 Neither do they that go by say, The blessing of Jehovah be upon you; We bless you in the name of Jehovah.

Psalm 130

A Song of Ascents.

1   Out of the depths have I cried unto thee, O Jehovah.

2   Lord, hear my voice: Let thine ears be attentive To the voice of my supplications.

3   If thou, Jehovah, shouldest mark iniquities, O Lord, who could stand?

4   But there is forgiveness with thee, That thou mayest be feared.

5   I wait for Jehovah, my soul doth wait, And in his word do I hope.

6   My soul waiteth for the Lord More than watchmen wait for the morning; Yea, more than watchmen for the morning.

7   O Israel, hope in Jehovah; For with Jehovah there is lovingkindness, And with him is plenteous redemption.

8   And he will redeem Israel From all his iniquities.

Psalm 131

A Song of Ascents; of David.

1. Jehovah, my heart is not haughty, nor mine eyes lofty; Neither do I exercise myself in great matters, Or in things too wonderful for me.

2. Surely I have stilled and quieted my soul; Like a weaned child with his mother, Like a weaned child is my soul within me.

3. O Israel, hope in Jehovah From this time forth and for evermore.

Psalm 132

A Song of Ascents.

1 Jehovah, remember for David All his affliction;

2 How he sware unto Jehovah, And vowed unto the Mighty One of Jacob:

3 Surely I will not come into the tabernacle of my house, Nor go up into my bed;

4 I will not give sleep to mine eyes, Or slumber to mine eyelids;

5 Until I find out a place for Jehovah, A tabernacle for the Mighty One of Jacob.

6 Lo, we heard of it in Ephrathah: We found it in the field of the wood.

7 We will go into his tabernacles; We will worship at his footstool.

8 Arise, O Jehovah, into thy resting-place; Thou, and the ark of thy strength.

9 Let thy priest be clothed with righteousness; And let thy saints shout for joy.

10 For thy servant David's sake Turn not away the face of thine anointed.

11 Jehovah hath sworn unto David in truth; He will not turn from it: Of the fruit of thy body will I set upon thy throne.

12 If thy children will keep my covenant And my testimony that I shall teach them, Their children also shall sit upon thy throne for evermore.

13 For Jehovah hath chosen Zion; He hath desired it for his habitation.

14   This is my resting-place for ever: Here will I dwell; for I have desired it.

15   I will abundantly bless her provision: I will satisfy her poor with bread.

16   Her priests also will I clothe with salvation; And her saints shall shout aloud for joy.

17   There will I make the horn of David to bud: I have ordained a lamp for mine anointed.

18   His enemies will I clothe with shame; But upon himself shall his crown flourish.

Psalm 133

A Song of Ascents; of David.

1   Behold, how good and how pleasant it is For brethren to dwell together in unity!

2   It is like the precious oil upon the head, That ran down upon the beard, Even Aaron's beard; That came down upon the skirt of his garments;

3   Like the dew of Hermon, That cometh down upon the mountains of Zion: For there Jehovah commanded the blessing, Even life for evermore.

Psalm 134

A Song of Ascents.

1   Behold, bless ye Jehovah, all ye servants of Jehovah, That by night stand in the house of Jehovah.

2   Lift up your hands to the sanctuary, And bless ye Jehovah.

3   Jehovah bless thee out of Zion; Even he that made heaven and earth.

Psalm 135

1 Praise ye Jehovah. Praise ye the name of Jehovah; Praise him, O ye servants of Jehovah,

2 Ye that stand in the house of Jehovah, In the courts of the house of our God.

3 Praise ye Jehovah; for Jehovah is good: Sing praises unto his name; for it is pleasant.

4 For Jehovah hath chosen Jacob unto himself, And Israel for his own possession.

5 For I know that Jehovah is great, And that our Lord is above all gods.

6 Whatsoever Jehovah pleased, that hath he done, In heaven and in earth, in the seas and in all deeps;

7 Who causeth the vapors to ascend from the ends of the earth; Who maketh lightnings for the rain; Who bringeth forth the wind out of his treasuries;

8 Who smote the first-born of Egypt, Both of man and beast;

9 Who sent signs and wonders into the midst of thee, O Egypt, Upon Pharaoh, and upon all his servants;

10 Who smote many nations, And slew mighty kings,

11 Sihon king of the Amorites, And Og king of Bashan, And all the kingdoms of Canaan,

12 And gave their land for a heritage, A heritage unto Israel his people.

13   Thy name, O Jehovah, endureth for ever; Thy memorial name, O Jehovah, throughout all generations.

14   For Jehovah will judge his people, And repent himself concerning his servants.

15   The idols of the nations are silver and gold, The work of men's hands.

16   They have mouths, but they speak not; Eyes have they, but they see not;

17   They have ears, but they hear not; Neither is there any breath in their mouths.

18   They that make them shall be like unto them; Yea, every one that trusteth in them.

19   O house of Israel, bless ye Jehovah: O house of Aaron, bless ye Jehovah:

20   O house of Levi, bless ye Jehovah: Ye that fear Jehovah, bless ye Jehovah.

21   Blessed be Jehovah out of Zion, Who dwelleth at Jerusalem. Praise ye Jehovah.

Psalm 136

1 Oh give thanks unto Jehovah; for he is good; For his lovingkindness endureth for ever.

2 Oh give thanks unto the God of gods; For his lovingkindness endureth for ever.

3 Oh give thanks unto the Lord of lords; For his lovingkindness endureth for ever:

4 To him who alone doeth great wonders; For his lovingkindness endureth for ever:

5 To him that by understanding made the heavens; For his lovingkindness endureth for ever:

6 To him that spread forth the earth above the waters; For his lovingkindness endureth for ever:

7 To him that made great lights; For his lovingkindness endureth for ever:

8 The sun to rule by day; For his lovingkindness endureth for ever;

9 The moon and stars to rule by night; For his lovingkindness endureth for ever:

10 To him that smote Egypt in their first-born; For his lovingkindness endureth for ever;

11 And brought out Israel from among them; For his lovingkindness endureth for ever;

12 With a strong hand, and with an outstretched arm; For his lovingkindness endureth for ever:

13   To him that divided the Red Sea in sunder; For his lovingkindness endureth for ever;

14   And made Israel to pass through the midst of it; For his lovingkindness endureth for ever;

15   But overthrew Pharaoh and his host in the Red Sea; For his lovingkindness endureth for ever:

16   To him that led his people through the wilderness; For his lovingkindness endureth for ever:

17   To him that smote great kings; For his lovingkindness endureth for ever;

18   And slew famous kings; For his lovingkindness endureth for ever:

19   Sihon king of the Amorites; For his lovingkindness endureth forever;

20   And Og king of Bashan; For his lovingkindness endureth for ever;

21   And gave their land for a heritage; For his lovingkindness endureth for ever;

22   Even a heritage unto Israel his servant; For his lovingkindness endureth for ever:

23   Who remembered us in our low estate; For his lovingkindness endureth for ever;

24   And hath delivered us from our adversaries; For his lovingkindness endureth for ever:

25   Who giveth food to all flesh; For his lovingkindness endureth for ever.

26   Oh give thanks unto the God of heaven; For his lovingkindness endureth for ever.

Psalm 137

1 By the rivers of Babylon, There we sat down, yea, we wept, When we remembered Zion.

2 Upon the willows in the midst thereof We hanged up our harps.

3 For there they that led us captive required of us songs, And they that wasted us required of us mirth, saying, Sing us one of the songs of Zion.

4 How shall we sing Jehovah's song In a foreign land?

5 If I forget thee, O Jerusalem, Let my right hand forget her skill.

6 Let my tongue cleave to the roof of my mouth, If I remember thee not; If I prefer not Jerusalem Above my chief joy.

7 Remember, O Jehovah, against the children of Edom The day of Jerusalem; Who said, Rase it, rase it, Even to the foundation thereof.

8 O daughter of Babylon, that art to be destroyed, Happy shall he be, that rewardeth thee As thou hast served us.

9 Happy shall he be, that taketh and dasheth thy little ones Against the rock.

Psalm 138

A Psalm of David.

1 I will give thee thanks with my whole heart: Before the gods will I sing praises unto thee.

2 I will worship toward thy holy temple, And give thanks unto thy name for thy lovingkindness and for thy truth: For thou hast magnified thy word above all thy name.

3 In the day that I called thou answeredst me, Thou didst encourage me with strength in my soul.

4 All the kings of the earth shall give thee thanks, O Jehovah, For they have heard the words of thy mouth.

5 Yea, they shall sing of the ways of Jehovah; For great is the glory of Jehovah.

6 For though Jehovah is high, yet hath he respect unto the lowly; But the haughty he knoweth from afar.

7 Though I walk in the midst of trouble, thou wilt revive me; Thou wilt stretch forth thy hand against the wrath of mine enemies, And thy right hand will save me.

8 Jehovah will perfect that which concerneth me: Thy lovingkindness, O Jehovah, endureth for ever; Forsake not the works of thine own hands.

Psalm 139

For the Chief Musician. A Psalm of David.

1   O Jehovah, thou hast searched me, and known me.

2   Thou knowest my downsitting and mine uprising; Thou understandest my thought afar off.

3   Thou searchest out my path and my lying down, And art acquainted with all my ways.

4   For there is not a word in my tongue, But, lo, O Jehovah, thou knowest it altogether.

5   Thou hast beset me behind and before, And laid thy hand upon me.

6   Such knowledge is too wonderful for me; It is high, I cannot attain unto it.

7   Whither shall I go from thy Spirit? Or whither shall I flee from thy presence?

8   If I ascend up into heaven, thou art there: If I make my bed in Sheol, behold, thou art there.

9   If I take the wings of the morning, And dwell in the uttermost parts of the sea;

10   Even there shall thy hand lead me, And thy right hand shall hold me.

11   If I say, Surely the darkness shall overwhelm me, And the light about me shall be night;

12   Even the darkness hideth not from thee, But the night shineth as the day: The darkness and the light are both alike to thee.

13   For thou didst form my inward parts: Thou didst cover me in my mother's womb.

14   I will give thanks unto thee; for I am fearfully and wonderfully made: Wonderful are thy works; And that my soul knoweth right well.

15   My frame was not hidden from thee, When I was made in secret, And curiously wrought in the lowest parts of the earth.

16   Thine eyes did see mine unformed substance; And in thy book they were all written, Even the days that were ordained for me, When as yet there was none of them.

17   How precious also are thy thoughts unto me, O God! How great is the sum of them!

18   If I should count them, they are more in number than the sand: When I awake, I am still with thee.

19   Surely thou wilt slay the wicked, O God: Depart from me therefore, ye bloodthirsty men.

20   For they speak against thee wickedly, And thine enemies take thy name in vain.

21   Do not I hate them, O Jehovah, that hate thee? And am not I grieved with those that rise up against thee?

22   I hate them with perfect hatred: They are become mine enemies.

23   Search me, O God, and know my heart: Try me, and know my thoughts;

24   And see if there be any wicked way in me, And lead me in the way everlasting.

Psalm 140

For the Chief Musician. A Psalm of David.

1   Deliver me, O Jehovah, from the evil man; Preserve me from the violent man:

2   Who devise mischiefs in their heart; Continually do they gather themselves together for war.

3   They have sharpened their tongue like a serpent; Adders' poison is under their lips. Selah

4   Keep me, O Jehovah, from the hands of the wicked; Preserve me from the violent man: Who have purposed to thrust aside my steps.

5   The proud have hid a snare for me, and cords; They have spread a net by the wayside; They have set gins for me. Selah

6   I said unto Jehovah, Thou art my God: Give ear unto the voice of my supplications, O Jehovah.

7   O Jehovah the Lord, the strength of my salvation, Thou hast covered my head in the day of battle.

8   Grant not, O Jehovah, the desires of the wicked; Further not his evil device, lest they exalt themselves. Selah

9   As for the head of those that compass me about, Let the mischief of their own lips cover them.

10 Let burning coals fall upon them: Let them be cast into the fire, Into deep pits, whence they shall not rise.

11 An evil speaker shall not be established in the earth: Evil shall hunt the violent man to overthrow him.

12 I know that Jehovah will maintain the cause of the afflicted, And justice for the needy.

13 Surely the righteous shall give thanks unto thy name: The upright shall dwell in thy presence.

Psalm 141

A Psalm of David.

1   Jehovah, I have called upon thee; make haste unto me: Give ear unto my voice, when I call unto thee.

2   Let my prayer be set forth as incense before thee; The lifting up of my hands as the evening sacrifice.

3   Set a watch, O Jehovah, before my mouth; Keep the door of my lips.

4   Incline not my heart to any evil thing, To practise deeds of wickedness With men that work iniquity: And let me not eat of their dainties.

5   Let the righteous smite me, it shall be a kindness; And let him reprove me, it shall be as oil upon the head; Let not my head refuse it: For even in their wickedness shall my prayer continue.

6   Their judges are thrown down by the sides of the rock; And they shall hear my words; for they are sweet.

7   As when one ploweth and cleaveth the earth, Our bones are scattered at the mouth of Sheol.

8   For mine eyes are unto thee, O Jehovah the Lord: In thee do I take refuge; leave not my soul destitute.

9   Keep me from the snare which they have laid for me, And from the gins of the workers of iniquity.

10 Let the wicked fall into their own nets, Whilst that I withal escape.

Psalm 142

Maschil of David, when he was in the cave; a Prayer.

1   I cry with my voice unto Jehovah; With my voice unto Jehovah do I make
supplication.

2   I pour out my complaint before him; I show before him my trouble.

3   When my spirit was overwhelmed within me, Thou knewest my path.
In the way wherein I walk Have they hidden a snare for me.

4   Look on my right hand, and see; For there is no man that knoweth me:
Refuge hath failed me; No man careth for my soul.

5   I cried unto thee, O Jehovah; I said, Thou art my refuge, My portion in
the land of the living.

6   Attend unto my cry; For I am brought very low: Deliver me from my
persecutors; For they are stronger than I.

7   Bring my soul out of prison, That I may give thanks unto thy name: The
righteous shall compass me about; For thou wilt deal bountifully with
me.

Psalm 143

A Psalm of David.

1 Hear my prayer, O Jehovah; give ear to my supplications: In thy faithfulness answer me, and in thy righteousness.

2 And enter not into judgment with thy servant; For in thy sight no man living is righteous.

3 For the enemy hath persecuted my soul; He hath smitten my life down to the ground: He hath made me to dwell in dark places, as those that have been long dead.

4 Therefore is my spirit overwhelmed within me; My heart within me is desolate.

5 I remember the days of old; I meditate on all thy doings; I muse on the work of thy hands.

6 I spread forth my hands unto thee: My soul thirsteth after thee, as a weary land. Selah

7 Make haste to answer me, O Jehovah; my spirit faileth: Hide not thy face from me, Lest I become like them that go down into the pit.

8 Cause me to hear thy lovingkindness in the morning; For in thee do I trust: Cause me to know the way wherein I should walk; For I lift up my soul unto thee.

9 Deliver me, O Jehovah, from mine enemies: I flee unto thee to hide me.

10 Teach me to do thy will; For thou art my God: Thy Spirit is good; Lead me in the land of uprightness.

11   Quicken me, O Jehovah, for thy name's sake: In thy righteousness bring
      my soul out of trouble.

12   And in thy lovingkindness cut off mine enemies, And destroy all them
      that afflict my soul; For I am thy servant.

Psalm 144

A Psalm of David.

1 Blessed be Jehovah my rock, Who teacheth my hands to war, And my fingers to fight:

2 My lovingkindness, and my fortress, My high tower, and my deliverer; My shield, and he in whom I take refuge; Who subdueth my people under me.

3 Jehovah, what is man, that thou takest knowledge of him? Or the son of man, that thou makest account of him?

4 Man is like to vanity: His days are as a shadow that passeth away.

5 Bow thy heavens, O Jehovah, and come down: Touch the mountains, and they shall smoke.

6 Cast forth lightning, and scatter them; Send out thine arrows, and discomfit them.

7 Stretch forth thy hand from above; Rescue me, and deliver me out of great waters, Out of the hand of aliens;

8 Whose mouth speaketh deceit, And whose right hand is a right hand of falsehood.

9 I will sing a new song unto thee, O God: Upon a psaltery of ten strings will I sing praises unto thee.

10 Thou art he that giveth salvation unto kings; Who rescueth David his servant from the hurtful sword.

11 Rescue me, and deliver me out of the hand of aliens, Whose mouth speaketh deceit, And whose right hand is a right hand of falsehood.

12 When our sons shall be as plants grown up in their youth, And our daughters as corner-stones hewn after the fashion of a palace;

13 When our garners are full, affording all manner of store, And our sheep bring forth thousands and ten thousands in our fields;

14 When our oxen are well laden; When there is no breaking in, and no going forth, And no outcry in our streets:

15 Happy is the people that is in such a case; Yea, happy is the people whose God is Jehovah.

Psalm 145

A Psalm of praise; of David.

1 I will extol thee, my God, O King; And I will bless thy name for ever and ever.

2 Every day will I bless thee; And I will praise thy name for ever and ever.

3 Great is Jehovah, and greatly to be praised; And his greatness is unsearchable.

4 One generation shall laud thy works to another, And shall declare thy mighty acts.

5 Of the glorious majesty of thine honor, And of thy wondrous works, will I meditate.

6 And men shall speak of the might of thy terrible acts; And I will declare thy greatness.

7 They shall utter the memory of thy great goodness, And shall sing of thy righteousness.

8 Jehovah is gracious, and merciful; Slow to anger, and of great lovingkindness.

9 Jehovah is good to all; And his tender mercies are over all his works.

10 All thy works shall give thanks unto thee, O Jehovah; And thy saints shall bless thee.

11 They shall speak of the glory of thy kingdom, And talk of thy power;

12 To make known to the sons of men his mighty acts, And the glory of the majesty of his kingdom.

13 Thy kingdom is an everlasting kingdom, And thy dominion endureth throughout all generations.

14 Jehovah upholdeth all that fall, And raiseth up all those that are bowed down.

15 The eyes of all wait for thee; And thou givest them their food in due season.

16 Thou openest thy hand, And satisfiest the desire of every living thing.

17 Jehovah is righteous in all his ways, And gracious in all his works.

18 Jehovah is nigh unto all them that call upon him, To all that call upon him in truth.

19 He will fulfil the desire of them that fear him; He also will hear their cry and will save them.

20 Jehovah preserveth all them that love him; But all the wicked will he destroy.

21 My mouth shall speak the praise of Jehovah; And let all flesh bless his holy name for ever and ever.

Psalm 146

1 Praise ye Jehovah. Praise Jehovah, O my soul.

2 While I live will I praise Jehovah: I will sing praises unto my God while I have any being.

3 Put not your trust in princes, Nor in the son of man, in whom there is no help.

4 His breath goeth forth, he returneth to his earth; In that very day his thoughts perish.

5 Happy is he that hath the God of Jacob for his help, Whose hope is in Jehovah his God:

6 Who made heaven and earth, The sea, and all that in them is; Who keepeth truth for ever;

7 Who executeth justice for the oppressed; Who giveth food to the hungry. Jehovah looseth the prisoners;

8 Jehovah openeth the eyes of the blind; Jehovah raiseth up them that are bowed down; Jehovah loveth the righteous;

9 Jehovah preserveth the sojourners; He upholdeth the fatherless and widow; But the way of the wicked he turneth upside down.

10 Jehovah will reign for ever, Thy God, O Zion, unto all generations. Praise ye Jehovah.

Psalm 147

1   Praise ye Jehovah; For it is good to sing praises unto our God; For it is pleasant, and praise is comely.

2   Jehovah doth build up Jerusalem; He gathereth together the outcasts of Israel.

3   He healeth the broken in heart, And bindeth up their wounds.

4   He counteth the number of the stars; He calleth them all by their names.

5   Great is our Lord, and mighty in power; His understanding is infinite.

6   Jehovah upholdeth the meek: He bringeth the wicked down to the ground.

7   Sing unto Jehovah with thanksgiving; Sing praises upon the harp unto our God,

8   Who covereth the heavens with clouds, Who prepareth rain for the earth, Who maketh grass to grow upon the mountains.

9   He giveth to the beast his food, And to the young ravens which cry.

10   He delighteth not in the strength of the horse: He taketh no pleasure in the legs of a man.

11   Jehovah taketh pleasure in them that fear him, In those that hope in his lovingkindness.

12   Praise Jehovah, O Jerusalem; Praise thy God, O Zion.

13   For he hath strengthened the bars of thy gates; He hath blessed thy children within thee.

14 He maketh peace in thy borders; He filleth thee with the finest of the wheat.

15 He sendeth out his commandment upon earth; His word runneth very swiftly.

16 He giveth snow like wool; He scattereth the hoar-frost like ashes.

17 He casteth forth his ice like morsels: Who can stand before his cold?

18 He sendeth out his word, and melteth them: He causeth his wind to blow, and the waters flow.

19 He showeth his word unto Jacob, His statutes and his ordinances unto Israel.

20 He hath not dealt so with any nation; And as for his ordinances, they have not known them. Praise ye Jehovah.

Psalm 148

1　Praise ye Jehovah. Praise ye Jehovah from the heavens: Praise him in the heights.

2　Praise ye him, all his angels: Praise ye him, all his host.

3　Praise ye him, sun and moon: Praise him, all ye stars of light.

4　Praise him, ye heavens of heavens, And ye waters that are above the heavens.

5　Let them praise the name of Jehovah; For he commanded, and they were created.

6　He hath also established them for ever and ever: He hath made a decree which shall not pass away.

7　Praise Jehovah from the earth, Ye sea-monsters, and all deeps.

8　Fire and hail, snow and vapor; Stormy wind, fulfilling his word;

9　Mountains and all hills; Fruitful trees and all cedars;

10　Beasts and all cattle; Creeping things and flying birds;

11　Kings of the earth and all peoples; Princes and all judges of the earth;

12　Both young men and virgins; Old men and children:

13　Let them praise the name of Jehovah; For his name alone is exalted; His glory is above the earth and the heavens.

14　And he hath lifted up the horn of his people, The praise of all his saints; Even of the children of Israel, a people near unto him. Praise ye Jehovah.

Psalm 149

1 Praise ye Jehovah. Sing unto Jehovah a new song, And his praise in the assembly of the saints.

2 Let Israel rejoice in him that made him: Let the children of Zion be joyful in their King.

3 Let them praise his name in the dance: Let them sing praises unto him with timbrel and harp.

4 For Jehovah taketh pleasure in his people: He will beautify the meek with salvation.

5 Let the saints exult in glory: Let them sing for joy upon their beds.

6 Let the high praises of God be in their mouth, And a two-edged sword in their hand;

7 To execute vengeance upon the nations, And punishments upon the peoples;

8 To bind their kings with chains, And their nobles with fetters of iron;

9 To execute upon them the judgment written: This honor have all his saints. Praise ye Jehovah.

Psalm 150

1   Praise ye Jehovah. Praise God in his sanctuary: Praise him in the firmament of his power.

2   Praise him for his mighty acts: Praise him according to his excellent greatness.

3   Praise him with trumpet sound: Praise him with psaltery and harp.

4   Praise him with timbrel and dance: Praise him with stringed instruments and pipe.

5   Praise him with loud cymbals: Praise him with high sounding cymbals.

6   Let everything that hath breath praise Jehovah. Praise ye Jehovah.

SUGGESTED READINGS

WARNING! REVELATION IS ABOUT TO BE FULFILLED by Larry W. Wilson *www.wake-up.org*

DISCOVERING ANCIENT PROPHECIES by Hilton Sutton Ph.D *www.hilton-sutton.org* & *www.asis.com/~stag/zodiac*

A DIVINE REVELATION OF HEAVEN by Mary K. Baxter

HE CAME TO SET THE CAPTIVES FREE by Rebecca Brown, MD

THE THREE BATTLEGROUNDS by Francis Frangipane

THE ROD OF IRON by Robert G. Barbaria
Note page 135 KING JAMES TRANSLATING the NAME YAHWEH into JE-HO'-VAH.

ABOUT THE ORGANIZATION

Trinity Ambassadors for Christ is a non-profit organization founded by Billie Jo Baldwin and her best friend, Donna Lynn Weill with the Heavenly Father's blessings for his one and only son, Jesus Christ by the Power of The Holy Spirit. The only way to Eternal Life is through Jesus Christ, to Him be all Power, Glory, and Honor.

Trinity Publishing is founded by Billie Jo Baldwin and Kosa, publishing the Good News of Jesus Christ through Music and Writing. Trinity Publishing has distributed writings, and poetry since it began in 2004 with God's blessings and the generosity of several people. Trinity is not affiliated or sponsored by any religious organization. Trinity Publishing does not have membership at this time. Its mission is John 3:14—Just as Moses lifted up the snake in the wilderness, so the SON OF MAN must be lifted up, so that everyone who believes in Him will have eternal life.

Also, its mission is to publish and proclaim the Good news of Jesus Christ through the Word of God and well defined Biblical Truths as in *http://www.god.tvRoryWendy/aganistAllOdds/, www.TBN.com & www.trinitysem.ed,* **www.newhopehealthclinic.com**, Dr. Bartell For Physical & Spiritual Healing, Jenks OK.

People off all faiths are encouraged to read the materials produced by Trinity Publishing.

We would very much like to receive comments about this book or questions you may have.

Thank you and God Bless.

Billie Jo Baldwin
P.O. Box 6593
Biloxi, MS 39540